MONOGRAPH NO. 40
AMERICAN ETHNOLOGICAL SOCIETY
Viola E. Garfield, Editor

Life in a Leyte Village

BY ETHEL NURGE

SEATTLE, 1965

University of Washington Press

Acknowledgments

Fig. 1. After Fred Eggan *et al.*, *Area Handbook on the Philippines*, University of Chicago for the Human Relations Area Files, 1956.

Fig. 8. After Beatrice B. Whiting (ed.), *Six Cultures: Studies of Child Rearing*, John Wiley and Sons, New York, 1963.

Preface

MOST of the data in this monograph are based on field work in Guinhangdan, a village in northeast Leyte, Philippines, in which I resided
from December, 1955, through July, 1956. I also spent the four
months prior to my arrival at the village in preliminary travel, survey, and study in the Philippines. In addition to the field work in the
village, data were abstracted from documentary sources and were
gathered through interviews from nonvillage personnel.[1]

The first chapter presents the general background material: the
influences shaping my choice of problem, the considerations affecting the choice of village, and the conditions of field work. In Chapter
1, I give the reasons for some of my choice-points. Chapter 2 describes the village setting. The mother-child investigation I wanted
to make required choosing mothers from a wide range of socioeconomic statuses to serve as my informants. To determine the categories, I conducted the investigations summarized in Chapter 3,
"Socioeconomic Structure." Chapter 4, "Household Composition,"
defines families. Chapter 5 concerns mothers and their children;
Chapter 6 discusses the role of women and other family members.

During my graduate work at Cornell University, I had become interested in the seminal studies of mother-child relationships and
their correlations with adult personality. No one denied that such
correlations existed, but the most useful theoretical and methodological tools to be used had not been, and are not yet, well fashioned
and widely accepted.

I had studied with William Lambert and worked with the *Field
Guide for a Study of Socialization in Five Societies*.[2] Plans were
then being made for the study of child-training practices in several

cultures. Six teams took the *Field Guide* into Mexico, New England, Okinawa, the Philippines, Kenya, and India. *Six Cultures: Studies of Child Rearing* is the fruitful result.[3] An important companion volume is promised.

Ideally, I should have been a member of one of those teams who went out to test the *Field Guide* and to gather the data for the statistical testing of the hypotheses. But I was not a team. Instead, I obtained a grant and went off on my own. What I did, technically, then, was to see to what extent the manual for the collection of data on socialization could guide and aid the work of a single investigator involved in the same subject as the teams. Therefore, the data I present here may be the subject of most useful comparison.

I have proceeded on the following assumptions: that the behavior systems emphasized in childhood will be both well learned and an important component in adult life; that the expression of these behavior systems will vary with sex, age, and socioeconomic position.

Some scientists will call these assumptions "hypotheses." And they well may be, depending on one's point of view, interests, and intentions. For the reader who wishes to consider what follows as data to test the hypotheses, these are the hypotheses. The discussion of the hypotheses begins in Chapter 5 and continues through 6. For those who will accept this monograph as a description with a minimum of inference, the inference is found on the same pages.

I consider the strength of this monograph to be in the careful attention to method and in the spelling out of much that is involved in method. I hope that these will be useful both for the reader and future fieldworkers. I consider my contribution to be the extension of the interview (Appendix I), designed for exploring mother-child interaction, to the exploration of mother-other relationships (Appendix II). Challenges and criticisms of the field work, the monograph, and the interpretation that I have put upon the data are welcome; nay, invited.

Contents

1: GENERAL CONSIDERATIONS
   CONCERNING CHOICE POINTS   3

2: THE SETTING   9

3: SOCIOECONOMIC STRUCTURE   23

4: HOUSEHOLD COMPOSITION   45

5: MOTHER AND CHILD IN GUINHANGDAN   64

6: DYADIC RELATIONSHIPS IN THE FAMILY   87

   APPENDIXES
   I. Schedule for Study of Mother-Child Relationship   131
   II. Schedule for Study of Dyadic Relationships of Women   140

   NOTES   141

   BIBLIOGRAPHY   148

   INDEX   151

Illustrations

PHOTOGRAPHS   *Facing*

An old woman, age 65   22
Woman's work: A typical wash day   22
An old-fashioned bamboo and nipa-thatched house   23
Women harvesting rice   23

MAPS

Map of Leyte   2
Map of Guinhangdan   11

FIGURES

1. Formal Philippine political structure and its relation
   to the political units   17
2. Floor plan of one of the larger houses   21
3. Household census sheet   46
4. Kinship chart   46
5. Extended horizontal family type   49
6. Extended vertical family type   49
7. Skipped generation extended vertical type   50
8. A simplified conceptual scheme for the study of
   patterns of child rearing and manifestations of
   personality characteristics   71

LIFE IN A LEYTE VILLAGE

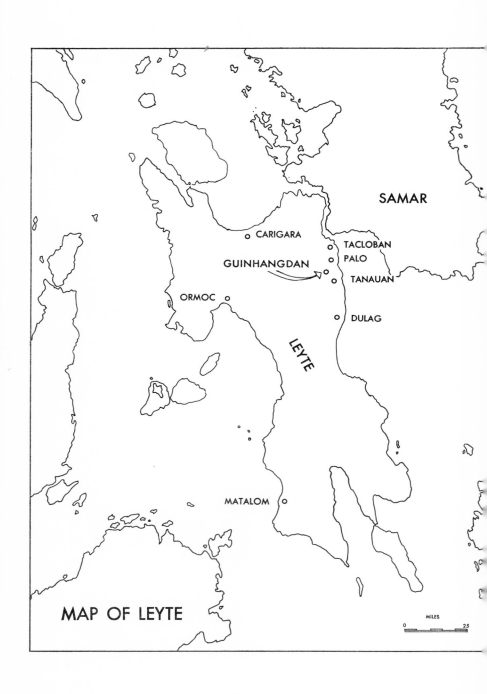

SAMAR

o CARIGARA

TACLOBAN
PALO

GUINHANGDAN

TANAUAN

ORMOC o

o DULAG

LEYTE

MATALOM o

MAP OF LEYTE

MILES

0   25

1: General Considerations Concerning Choice Points

CHOICE OF A VILLAGE

SELECTING a village was difficult for me and entailed a number of considerations. In my preliminary surveys in the Philippines, I had been attracted to agricultural-fishing villages. For personal and ascetic reasons, I should have liked a village almost wholly dependent upon fishing, but such villages are relatively rare. In many instances, the economic structure of a village is important for the research design, but for the subjects in which I was interested the economic make-up had a delimitable relationship which could be taken into consideration.

I chose this particular agricultural-fishing village because, first of all, it appealed to me. Second, Guinhangdan — the name has been changed in this study — was not devoted only to agriculture, but to agriculture and fishing combined, which meant that information could be obtained concerning several different kinds of families.

In the year that I went into the field, Philippine studies were beginning to show the fruits of the lifelong interest and investigations of Fred Eggan. His own work, his students (I am one), and the formation of his Philippine Studies Program have culminated in a series of studies whose diversity, vigor, and strength owe much to him. In the year 1955–56, an unusual number of investigators (about half a dozen of whom were professional anthropologists and the majority of whom were either graduate students or recent Ph.D.'s) had recently been in, or were soon to be in, the Philippines for their field work. No systematic anthropological investigation had been undertaken in the Visayan Islands. I chose this area because the whole

3

region lay unexplored and anything I could find would be of interest, heightened by the fact that so little was known.

Having chosen the Visayans because they were untouched, why did I choose Leyte? The choice came about through one of those accidents that guide our choices more frequently than we recognize. A student friend at Cornell University came from a wealthy American-Filipino family in Tacloban. For her sake, I was welcomed to Tacloban, shown much hospitality, introduced to important people, and helped in many ways. I began to search intensively in the Tacloban area and found Guinhangdan.

For research purposes, it was desirable that a village be small enough to permit a single investigator to come to know it well in the time available for the field study. Some of the information to be sought was quantitative. I had no machine facilities for counting and sorting and planned to collect items that could be tallied by hand. This procedure automatically limited the number of people with whom it was possible to work.

For the most efficient use of time, it was best that the homes be in rather close proximity to each other and not spread out over a wide area as were the residences in some villages I had considered previously. An added advantage was that living in a dense cluster of houses gave me access to many facets of daily life which could not have become known by the resident with more privacy and isolation.

On the other hand, there was reason to seek a village that was not too small, because it was necessary to find a population large enough to ensure a fair number of children in the three-to-ten age group.

Other considerations affecting the choice of the village were not related to research design or field method but to the convenience and comfort of the investigator. I had no private transportation and I wanted access to public transportation. Therefore I chose a village on the National Road, a two-lane highway which was paved for the most part and ran north and south on the east coast of Leyte. Public buses ran on this road.

ANOTHER SERIES OF CHOICE POINTS: DATA COLLECTION

Paradoxically, when one is in the field, the haunting question is not what data *to* collect but what data *not* to collect. The problem is not one of assemblage but one of selective elimination. Much of the myriad visual, auditory, and, sometimes, olfactory stimuli that impinge on the investigator cannot be recorded. In the exciting experience of living in a new culture, so much is illuminating and significant that one is constantly faced with the problem of how to choose among the experiences of sixteen wakeful hours for those events and impressions that will become part of the recorded data.

In regard to the selection of experience to be observed and recorded, it is worth noting that, in the first weeks in the field, the anthropologist is particularly impressionable. All that he sees before him which is different from that which he knows from his own society strikes him with force. There is drama in the living of these days and a clarity of perception about easily observable actions which are later dulled. It was frustrating that not all the novelty could be recorded while it was pristine. Too soon the exotic became commonplace and little details, which had been memorable at first, became not worthy of note. Too soon, that which initially was strange became routine.

The extent of my immersion in the village society became clear when Hollywood visitors came toward the end of my stay and, in the process of helping them to get certain pictures, I had a chance to see Americans exposed for the first time to Philippine village society. It was a revealing situation. When they reveled in the color of a fighting cock and delighted to see it carried to the cockpit in an outrigger canoe, their reaction illuminated how the exotic had become commonplace to me. Their reaction made me aware of changes in my attitude and behavior from the days when I too was a newcomer in the village. The diffidence with which they spoke to my Filipino friends recalled to me my own early ignorance, caution, and hesitant approach. Now I spoke quickly and freely, with a high degree of certainty as to what the answers would be before they came. This deep immersion in, and understanding of, local customs, beliefs, habits, and ways of thinking is the anthropologist's special knowledge and strength.

The data were selected in accordance with the canons of accepted anthropological procedure. Social and educational leaders were sought out and after a few weeks of residence a household census was begun. General knowledge on a score of nonthreatening subjects was elicited and genealogies were constructed. A map was secured. As the personalities and capabilities of individual people became clearer, key informants were chosen for interviews in their specialties. At the same time, an intensive series of interviews were planned for twenty-five mothers who were to be carefully picked according to certain criteria. In order to select the mothers, it was necessary to know something of socioeconomic levels. Information was gathered and analysis of land ownership, occupation, and income data was begun. At this point, we were already in the fourth month of the project. Twenty-five mothers proved to be too large a sample to be handled and the number was reduced to twelve. The information gathering continued until the end of the project.

A problem separate from the selection of the data to be recorded was the actual recording. How should the recording be done? Although an assistant and I spent several hours every day compiling typewritten records, the portion of our experience that actually got into the notes was a small part of the whole, an inevitable limitation in field work. Exact working procedures for collecting and recording each section of the data will be described later.

In regard to my role, I was introduced to the village as a teacher from America who wanted to study about Philippine history and customs. The reception accorded me was cordial and I was housed with a young, prominent couple, both of whom were teachers in the elementary school. He taught mechanical training and she taught home economics. Also resident in the house were his two sons from a previous marriage which had been terminated by death. Of these four individuals, I most frequently saw the wife. We often visited and chatted. Less frequently I saw the husband, who, because of the rules concerning male-female relationships, never came without his wife. The two sons were not permitted by their parents to enter my section of the house, but living in close proximity to them afforded some glimpses of family life not otherwise possible.

CHOICE OF ASSISTANTS

Throughout my stay in the field I was aided constantly by two resourceful girls, my assistants in the fullest sense of the word. Both girls came from good families, were in their late twenties, were unmarried, and possessed more education than most girls in the village. They were cheerful and cooperative and had considerable ability. I trained them and they "trained" me.

Both girls were told as much of the aims of the study as was compatible with their understanding. They received some instruction from me in information-eliciting techniques and worked to teach me some of the language. We also gained practice and facility by translating material from the dialect into English, or from English into the dialect. It is, perhaps, not often enough stressed that training is a two-way road. I learned much as I endeavored to teach my assistants how to help me.

Aside from language and information-gathering training, there was other work to be shared. I taught one girl to type, for our record-keeping was extensive and it was necessary for two of us to type a few hours each day. All the formal interviewing was done with the help of one or both of these girls. In addition, much of the informal visiting and casual, everyday prying was done in their company. And, finally, they often acted as informants on matters of local interest in which they were well versed.

I attempted two lengthy interviews a day. Many days I achieved only one. The interviews were administered in English or Waray Waray, according to a prior decision. (Administration techniques are described in the body of the text inasmuch as they differed from time to time according to the method being used.) I wrote down the information elicited in both shorthand and longhand. Shorthand seemed more practical and I should have liked to have taken everything verbatim, but a system of notation for the material being gathered was not fully worked out. The shorthand system of notation devised in Western culture primarily for use in business letters and similar transactions proved not entirely practical when recording conversation, probes, and disconnected explanations. The material was transcribed as soon as possible after an interview. In addition to lengthy interviews which were recorded on the spot, shorter ones were recorded from memory soon after the talk took place.

To supplement the interview material, I wrote notes on observations made daily. Every day I walked around the village at least once, chatting and visiting. Almost every afternoon I went out on the river in an outrigger canoe, sometimes up the river to the farms, sometimes down the river to the ocean. The information gained on these trips was also included in the typed records.

Again, let me repeat that the fieldworker faces a constant problem both of selection in perception and of selection in recording. A good deal is lost through cultural misconceptions and because we are not giant recording machines. A phenomenon happening before us has to pass through selective filters of eyes, ears, brain, and experience. Then it is further extracted, abstracted, and funneled as it is channeled into a notebook and finally distilled on a card. Finally, at the end of the field term, the investigator takes home the card file and a host of unrecorded memories and impressions and the arduous work of analysis begins.

2: The Setting

SOUTHEAST of China, due east of Vietnam, and north of Borneo and Australia lie the Philippine Islands. The northernmost point of Luzon is close to nineteen degrees latitude; in the south, the Tawi Tawi Group of the Sulu Archipelago are located about five degrees north of the equator.[1] From Manila one may fly north to Hongkong, Formosa, and Japan. To the east, the nearest neighbors are in the Mariana and Caroline islands but these are fifteen hundred miles away. To the south, from Mindanao, it is but a watery step to Borneo; smugglers and traders in their small wind- and man-powered craft cross regularly.

Most of the more than seven thousand islands in the Philippines are mere rocks; only a little over a hundred islands are inhabited. The total land area is 115,600 square miles. Population is distributed unequally but averages one hundred seventy-one persons per square mile. Most of the islands have a backbone of mountain ranges; coastal ranges are found on others. Nowhere are the mountains very high; the loftiest peak is Mount Apo in Mindanao, at 9,450 feet.[2] Generally the mountains fall off sharply in interior plains and plateaus. The depths around the Philippines are more impressive than are the heights. Off to the southeast are the greatest depths ever to be recorded; here the sea bottom descends to 35,410 feet.[3]

Rainfall varies from area to area, depending on such features as position relevant to the next land mass, prevailing winds, currents, and elevation. There are no seasons other than wet and dry, as a general rule, although in the extreme north it is cooler in winter. Two resort areas, Baguio on Luzon and Bukidnon on Mindanao, are cool because of their plateau elevation. Typhoons and earthquakes are known in the islands but the earthquakes are but slight tremors whereas the typhoons are often violent, particularly in the central and northern islands.

The islands containing the largest land mass are Luzon in the north and Mindanao in the south. The Philippines may be divided into the northern, central, and southern groups and of these we shall be concerned with the central or Visayan Islands. Here are Panay, Negros, Cebu, Leyte, Samar, and Bohol, reading from west to east. A village in east Leyte is our focus.

HISTORY OF THE VILLAGE

Guinhangdan nestles in the loop of a river that winds around to the north, east, and west. Periodically, the marshy and swampy areas that line the banks are scoured by flood waters. Coconut and nipa palms are planted in the fertile black sandy river banks. Other crops are planted in fields away from the village and are reached by a short journey in an outrigger canoe, or by walking through the marshes or woods. Within the village, a small amount of land is used for gardens. A quarter of a mile to the east, past shallow stretches of the river and some sand bars is Leyte Gulf.

A plane from Manila flies over the village every other day. Seen from the air, Guinhangdan presents a quickly glimpsed panorama of road, river, sea, huts, houses, and vegetation. The national road, which was under construction and repair for the length of my stay, runs north and south through the village. Traveling north two kilometers, one reaches another village; next, one arrives at Palo, the municipal center; and, finally, Tacloban, the provincial capital, which is seventeen kilometers away. Traveling south three kilometers, one comes to the fair-sized town of Tanauan with its market and cockpit. However, the markets and cockpits of Palo and Tacloban are more frequently visited by the people of Guinhangdan than are those of Tanauan.

Coming into the village from the north by foot, bus, or jeep, one crosses the bridge over the river, walks past a marshy swamp lined with heavy vegetation, and enters the area of residence. The houses stretch for a kilometer north and south, becoming sparse to the south. East and west, the streets and paths stretch half a kilometer to the banks of the river and creeks.

The village is built in a rough grid pattern around a plaza con-

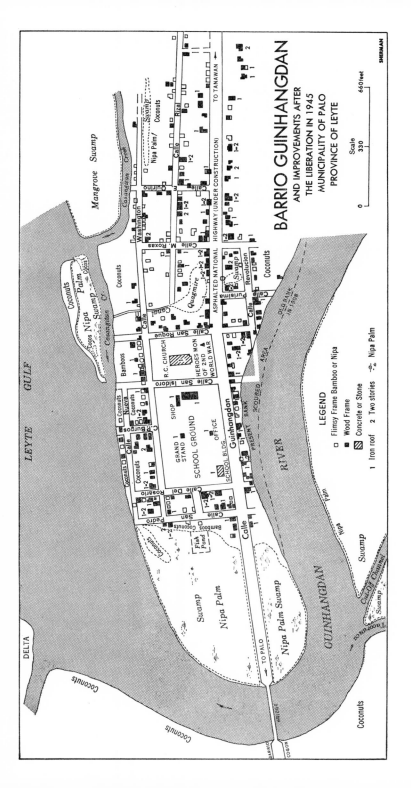

BARRIO GUINHANGDAN
AND IMPROVEMENTS AFTER
THE LIBERATION IN 1945
MUNICIPALITY OF PALO
PROVINCE OF LEYTE

SHERMAN

Scale
0   330   660 feet

LEGEND

□ Flimsy Frame Bamboo or Nipa
■ Wood Frame
▨ Concrete or Stone
1 Iron roof   2 Two stories
⌐ⁿ Nipa Palm

LEYTE GULF

DELTA

Coconuts

Mangrove Swamp

Casaagitan Creek

Nipa Palm/
Coconuts

Nipa Palm Swamp
Cogon

Coconuts

Cesagitan Cr.

Coconuts

Washington

Quirino

Calle Rizal

Calle

Calle M. Roxas

HIGHWAY (UNDER CONSTRUCTION)

TO TANAWAN

Swamp

Coconuts

ASPHALTED NATIONAL

Quagmire

Swamp

Calle Revolucion

Purisima

Calle

Coconuts

Grand

Calle

Calle San Roque

Bamboos

R.C. CHURCH

HEROES MON
OF 2ND
WORLD WAR

Calle San Isidoro

Guinhangdan

SHOP

Coconuts

Calle Nueva

Sobing

Calle

GRAND
STAND

SCHOOL GROUND

OFFICE

SCHOOL BLDG.

PRESENT BANK

OLD BANK
IN 1918

SCOURED
AREA

RIVER

Coconuts

Calle Rosario

Calle Del

Calle San Pedro

Fish
Pond

Bamboos

Coconuts

Coconuts

Calle

Palm

Nipa

Swamp

Swamp

Nipa Palm

Swamp

Nipa Palm Swamp

GUINHANGDAN

Cut-Off Channel

Swamp

TO PALO

BARRIO
COGON
BRIDGE

Coconuts

Coconuts

Coconuts

taining the school and church grounds. Houses are placed at irregular intervals and at irregular distances from the walks. Only the national road is paved and it is on this road that 99 per cent of the vehicular traffic passes.

There are no electrical or fire-fighting facilities. Water is procured from wells, although a few households have tapped a spur line from a reservoir to the south that services Tacloban. Mail is delivered once a week but any outgoing mail must be carried to the Palo post office.

The origin of the village is lost in the mists of time.[4] In the early decades of the Spanish occupation, priests were sent to the provinces to establish churches and parishes. In Guinhangdan, this meant that the priest and his representatives visited farm owners and tenants scattered along the river exhorting the people to accept the new religion and to "live under the bell." To "live under the bell" meant to establish residence in a locale which had as its center a church and a plaza. According to the earliest accounts available, a hamlet (*sitio*) stood where the village (*barrio*) now is.

Many of the first immigrants came from an inland farm area known as Bunga. In the memory of living informants, comparatively recent attempts have been made to increase the village population by inviting nearby farmers to come in with their families and settle. As an incentive, the *emigrés* were given a small amount of land for house building. About fifty families accepted this opportunity and moved into the village around the turn of the century. Another increment to population in the same period was the arrival of five families of Tagalogs from Cavite who fled Luzon following unrest and revolution on that island in 1898.[5] The final increment to population is of a temporary nature. In 1948, some young unmarried adult males were brought into the village to pursue a special and dangerous industry. Their stay is limited; they have learned a little Waray Waray, but none of them has married, or intends to marry, into the village.

Few people living today remember life under the Spanish. It was their administrative practice to establish one of the villagers as a local official whose duty was to collect a head tax of two pesos for every person over eighteen in the village. The tax collector made such a collection every year and turned the money over to the mayor (*capitan*) of the village, who in turn checked the sum against a list to see that all who were eligible for assessment had paid. If, as was all too often the case, someone was too poor to pay the assessment, the tax collector was expected to pay for him! Acceptance of appointment of office of tax collector was obligatory, and as the period of tenure was uncertain, a man of wealth was chosen for the position. "A village treasurer after serving for many years always became poor." In addition to the head tax, a system of forced labor (*catanod*) was levied on the people. The work parties so recruited cleaned the undergrowth from the paths, dredged the shallow river ways, and built rude bridges. Education consisted of the teaching of prayers, catechism, and the letters of the alphabet.

The Spanish rule of the islands lasted until the Spanish-American War brought changes in 1898. After some indecision, the United States of America accepted the task of administering the Philippines. Among the more noteworthy achievements of the American occupation forces was the establishment of schools. Four decades of slow cultural change passed. The Philippines were being prepared for democratic independence when, in 1941, the dramatic attacks of the Japanese on Pearl Harbor and Luzon changed the course of events.

Although the Japanese attacked the northern Philippines in December, 1941, they did not get to Leyte until the following May. They landed at Carigara and marched into supine Tacloban, the provincial capital. Most Filipinos were prepared to meet the conquerors with a smile, gifts of fruit and fish, and patience. There was the usual gamut of cooperative people, the uninterested, the fearful, and the resistance fighters. In the beginning, the number of resistance fighters was so small as to be unimportant. However, the more daring and hardy of these took to the hills and began to organize in a tentative fashion. As the resistance fighters organized into bands, the stay-at-home villagers found themselves caught between the pressure exerted by the Japanese occupation troops and that of their own guerrillas. Neither side, understandably, wanted to see the other supported or aided. The peasant, in the manner of peasants immemorial, was afraid of both, wished they would leave him alone, and did his daily self-effacing best to get along with both. "If we stay in the village, the guerrillas are angry; if we go into the mountains, the Japanese are angry."

The Japanese set up an organization called "Neighborhood," which was to recruit workers to help build trenches, make ropes and nets, and build bridges. Another organization called "Kalibapi" seems to have been a committee for collaboration or cooperation between the Japanese and the Filipinos. Officials were appointed, helpers designated, and, rather reluctantly, the Filipinos assumed the new roles urged on them by the establishment of the Kalibapi.

Schools in the village were closed. Life went on much as it had except for sporadic visits from Japanese. There were fields to plant and harvest, and fish to be caught. Buying and selling continued, but gradually the galling presence of an invasion army in the homeland, coupled with the cruelty of some Japanese, markedly increased sympathy for the guerrillas. Often the Japanese arrived for a surprise inspection and interrogation; they indulged in malicious teasing, spiteful goading, insult, and injury. Food and clothing were requisitioned and sometimes paid for. "Camotes are for the Japanese; you will eat sand," said one ruthless patrol leader and his words were bitterly remembered. When the Japanese arrested guerrilla suspects, or known contacts of friends of guerrillas, they tortured them. Some prisoners were decapitated and their heads stuck on poles in the market place. Sometimes a village was set on fire. The villagers reacted by constructing hideaway huts in the swamps and near the mountains and gradually the village was deserted by all except the old people. The ranks of the guerrillas swelled and their support became more general and more popular.

Although the Americans had been dealt a crushing defeat, most Filipinos thought they would come back. In the years that followed the fall of Corregidor and the death march of Bataan, the Filipinos speculated about the return of the Americans. In August, 1944, harbingers of the liberation arrived in Guinhangdan in two forms. An American submarine sent ashore maps, cigarettes, and gum; and a newspaper called *Free Philippines* began to make its appearance. About the middle of September, the village people had their first experience with American bombs. Light planes bombed the coast and continued the bombardment intermittently for the next month. Incendiary bombs were dropped on the better homes, some of which the Japanese had commandeered. Various installations were damaged, coconut trees were broken off or burned, and Filipinos found themselves in a familiar position, this time caught in the cross fire of the Japanese and the Americans.

Late in October, the American liberation forces landed. The native food supply was low but rice farming had been maintained. There was a shortage of clothing and drugs, commodities brought in good quantity by the Americans. Today the liberation is remembered as a time of prosperity and plenty. To the astonishment of the natives, ton after ton of supplies was brought ashore by the liberation army. Food, cigarettes, clothing, and gum were liberally distributed for many months. The American soldiers, known as GI's, were generous spenders and did not cavil at high prices. For the most part, the troops were neither condescending nor derogatory in their dealings with Filipinos. Americans today (1956) have high prestige in Leyte villages and some of the credit for this standing must be given to a show of strength and resources, and to the conduct of the officers and men of the task force both during and after the liberation.

Most of the villages of northeastern Leyte were occupied. The nearby village of Gocan had a hospital, and Guinhangdan, a post office, snack bar, and a finance office. The school was reopened and many children attended. The army, needing washerwomen, laborers, and other workers, provided jobs for many. Food, clothing, and money "flowed like rain to everyone," according to one enraptured informant. The effects of that honeymoon were still visible at the time of the field work.

In July, 1945, the Republic of the Philippines was established. What this meant to the villager needs to be assessed. It is doubtful that he was impressed. "We have been freed three times," said an informant cynically, referring to the 1898 revolt against the Spanish, the "self-government" of puppets set up by the Japanese, and the formation of the Republic in 1945.

POLITICAL ORGANIZATION

Living in the Republic means that the villager is subject to laws on the municipal, provincial, and national levels. Fig. 1 depicts the interlocking relationships of the various agencies and levels. A few definitions are in order.

A municipality is an area of political jurisdiction. It includes a town or *población* from which the area is administered and all barrios or villages in the area and the fields or uncultivated land therein. (A unit smaller than a village is a sitio or a settlement of hamlet size.) Some confusion in the use of the term barrio is noted by Romani:

The term barrio is employed to describe any and all sub-units of the municipalities which lie outside the poblacion (municipal center) as well as subdivisions of some of the smaller chartered cities. This double use of the term leads to confusion, for the rural barrio differs considerably from a barrio located within an urban or semi-urban area. The latter closely resembles a ward or precinct in a small American city, while the former is more akin to the prototype of an Asian village.[6]

Guinhangdan is a rural barrio under the jurisdiction of the town of Palo which in turn has its own wardlike barrios. According to Rivera and McMillan, the average barrio has approximately two hundred to two hundred and fifty families and from fifteen to sixteen hundred people.[7] Guinhangdan fits well within these limits, having two hundred and sixty families (households) and about twelve hundred people.

According to Romani, the present formal barrio government is a result of the development of Spanish and American modifications on the indigenous social and political unit. The first Filipinos of Malayan origin came in extended family groups whose leaders were chiefs and elders. At first, the Spanish worked with this unit and permitted the leader to retain his authority and function. Gradually, an extended family group of elders and chief became part of a reorganized unit of several extended families. In the process of reorganization, the barrio came into being and the chief became the barrio *teniente* (lieutenant).

The Americans made few changes in the local government unit. The barrio continued as a subdivision of the town or municipality and the barrio teniente was the chief administrative officer of the village.[8] Guinhangdan has a teniente, two vice-lieutenants or subtenientes, and three councilmen. Collectively, they are known as the council. Village officials are appointed by the town (población) councilmen and serve without pay but they do receive per diem when attending meetings.

Despite the formality of the structure, real government is lacking on the village level. The unsalaried lieutenant and the councilmen are little more than advisers to the villagers. They mediate in quarrels and act as liaison to important visitors. But they are not authorized to levy taxes, or to provide for roads, schools, or other facilities. The school system is maintained by the national government; teachers are provided through the national Department of Education and are paid from national funds. So, too, health services are rendered by a municipal and national government office and the district agricultural officer is both a local and a national official.[9]

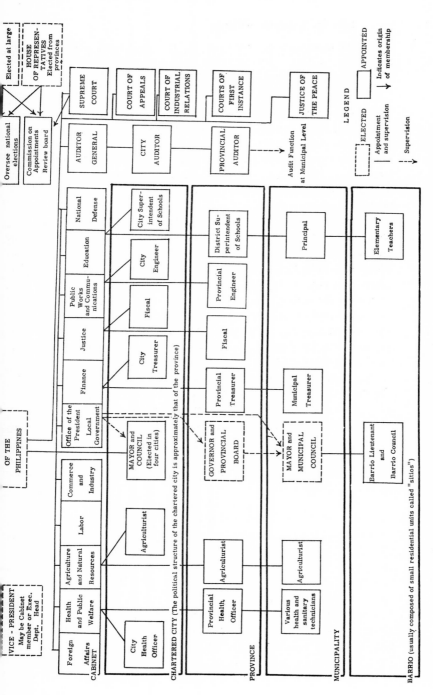

Fig. 1. Formal Philippine political structure and its relation to the political units.

No health, education, or agricultural officer is resident in Guin-hangdan, although several elementary school teachers are.

The average villager has few contacts with the municipal government. The municipal government obtains revenues from land tax and taxes on certain occupations and businesses but most revenue comes from allotments from the national government. Each villager is liable for a residence tax. Those who own livestock or land are liable for the personal and real property tax. Residents go to Palo to pay taxes, to use the post office, and to report births, deaths, civil disturbances, or criminal acts to the authorities.

Another indication that the barrio lacks a real local government is the lack of a police force. Public opinion remains the strongest deterrent to antisocial behavior. The ideal official has qualities which compensate for the lack of a constabulary. Any officer may be called upon to mediate in quarrels and should have the qualities of a peacemaker as well as being a model of decorum himself.

All village officials should be able to read and write, be reasonable and mild of temper. Their bearing and manner should convey sincerity and command respect. Sibley has hypothesized that a barrio councilman must possess a combination of four qualities: numerous consanguineal and affinal kin, wealth or land which make it probable that he will have many contacts outside of the barrio, nominal religious participation, preferably, but not necessarily, Catholic; and relatively great biological-social age.[10] In general, councilmen in Guinhangdan do have these characteristics. The one apparent exception proved the rule rather than the reverse. One teniente met all the other qualifications but was unusually young and, partly in consequence, failed to be as persuasive or effective as the other officials.

PROTECTION FROM THE ELEMENTS: CLOTHING AND HOUSING

Although protection from the elements is only one function of clothing and housing, it is a convenient and not misleading category under which to discuss both. Both personal covering and residence provide privacy to a degree and of a kind. Both also are indicators of social status and attainment.

Before the introduction of the Spanish loom and the importing of cloth, most clothing was made of abaca. Abaca cloth is stiff and coarse and is prepared by a tedious process from the same plant from which rope is made. None is manufactured today in Guinhangdan and elsewhere in the islands the craft is dying out. Women wore a long skirt of abaca fiber gathered at the waist with a string and topped this with a loose, short, wide-necked, loose-sleeved blouse. Men wore abaca shirts, and knee-length pants or ankle-length trousers. Both sexes owned fancier items for church, visits, and ceremonial occasions.

Clothing today is strongly affected by American and European styles which reach the native populace in a number of ways. Probably the most common influences are American or European missionaries, teachers, resident priests, government, or medical personnel. A further influence is American movies, which are imported regularly and in great numbers, and are exhibited in any town of sufficient size to have an electric and ice-producing plant. The village has no movie; Palo has none; but Tacloban has four. Finally, the importing and selling of used American clothing is an industry of unexpected proportions.

Yet, despite the fact that both used and new ready-to-wear American clothing are held to be of superior quality and styling to any of the products made at home or by Filipino dressmakers and tailors, most clothing is made at home from materials from the Ilocos area of Luzon, from Iloilo (a port city in Panay), from Japan, or America. The cloth has prestige value in the order of the places listed, American being most valued. Abaca clothing is still worn by the old people and, occasionally, by others for heavier work. *Timasa* or work clothes are soiled, stained, or worn garments which are worn for farming, fishing, or heavy labor. The well-to-do, of course, own more clothes of better quality than do the poor people who make up the majority. But since great value is vested in a good appearance, even the most poverty-stricken peasant strives to have at least one outfit of sartorial elegance. Fancier clothes and special dress items are necessary for school, church, visits, dances, baptisms, weddings, funerals, memorial services, and fiestas.

Infants and toddlers wear only an undershirt. Children of school age usually go about without underwear but are otherwise clad in cotton dresses or shirts and pants not unlike summer clothing in America. Adult females wear cotton dresses and adult males wear shirts and trousers.

There is no seasonal variation in clothing. The climate is humid and warm or hot throughout the year but it is wetter in the rainy season. No special rain clothing is worn although umbrellas are a symbol of wealth among women who can afford them. Children may also use umbrellas but adult males do not. If caught in a downpour, a man may cut a few feet of tough protective banana leaf and shelter under that while walking. Old-style woven hats, which mark the rural person from the city dweller, are useful for rain wear in the village although they would not be worn to town except by the most humble and unpretentious.

Several types of footgear prevail. Children normally go barefoot, the boys persisting in this habit longer than the girls. The common type of footwear both for children getting their first shoes, and for adults, is the *bakia*, which consists of a wooden sole with a wide strip attached transversely. Today the strip is often made of celluloid but a wide variety of materials is used. The bakia is cheap, durable, and practical. One may slosh in and out of puddles, shuffle across streams, sit with feet in the often flooded bottom of an outrigger canoe, and all the shoe needs is some drying. On coming to the residence, one slips off the bakia at the entrance and walks barefoot in the house. Bakias, like the old-style woven hats, are disdained by some people but are too practical not to be used even when they have become a derogated symbol of the poor. In town, it is the "bakia crowd," the poor and simple tenant farmer or laborer, who vociferously enjoys the Western, jungle, or horror films. Imported Western shoes are sometimes used but they are expensive. On other islands, local manufacture of the Western footwear is now being undertaken. Bakias are made in the village. Slippers, made of abaca, are a specialization of certain villages.

As for housing, residences are generally one-story structures raised off the ground and supported on heavy posts. The section between the posts and under the house, the *sirong*, is generally not enclosed. Here the children may play, unused items be laid, or a corner penned off for the nighttime care of the livestock. The enclosed section of the house where the family sleep, eat, or live that portion of their life which they spend indoors (considerably less than with Americans) may be one small room or several. The larger houses may be extended by outside platforms and porches. The area around the house and sometimes under the house is a working area. Trees, a flimsy roof, or the shadow of a building may shelter the worker. If the house in on the river, the outrigger canoe is beached nearby. The bigger canoes owned by the wealthy may have roof shelters. Another kind of outbuilding is the *sari sari* store, a small, four-sided, roofed structure which faces the path or road. The façade includes a counter topped by removable half-walls or windows. There are no other outbuildings with the exception of the occasional, little-used pit latrines. A well dug near a house is shared by several households.

In the main, houses are constructed of bamboo and nipa palm, the latter being sewn into thatches for walling and roofing. Bamboo and nipa houses are nontaxable, whereas those utilizing wood or a galvanized tin roof are taxable. As is true of other material goods, the older, indigenous style — the nipa and bamboo — is both more practical and comfortable, and carries less prestige.

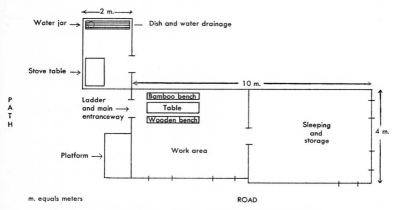

Fig. 2. Floor plan of one of the larger houses.

The number of rooms and the floor plan itself varies considerably but certain basic features are always found. The same area may serve many purposes if space is limited. Sleeping mats are simply unrolled on the floor at night and taken up and placed in the rafters during the day. There is no sink but a large water jug stands on a platform. Nearby is a cooking platform containing a bed of sand and a stand for the pots. Furniture is minimal, usually including a table with an accompanying bench. The family may boast a chair or two. In some houses the sleeping mat may be replaced by a woven hammock. The families in the best financial position may have quite elaborate furniture, including a living room set of a number of wooden, cane-bottomed chairs, couch, potted plants, and anachronistic antimacassars.

Fig. 2 provides a floor plan for one of the larger houses. An altar — often a little shelf in a corner on which are placed religious paraphernalia — is nearly always part of a Guinhangdan village home. Cheap colored pictures, sold by traveling salesmen and in the local markets, may adorn a wall. Figures of saints are rare but a candle, paper flowers, or a medal may serve as tokens to remind the household of the required obedience and submission to an all-powerful protective pantheon.

Visiting customs ensure a modicum of privacy in a setting where privacy is minimal. When approaching a household, it is customary for the visitor to stand well away from the entranceway and cheerily murmur the greeting appropriate to the time of the day. If the house is obviously closed, with the door and windows covered and the ladder drawn up, one should not approach at all. If the visitor is welcome, the householder will call "Good," or "Come up." One always goes "up" a house in Guinhangdan not "in" or "into" which, considering the raised construction, is logical.

We have been concerned with the history of an agricultural-fishing village in northeastern Leyte. In summary, despite more than three hundred years of Spanish influence, fifty years of American influence, and some few years of occupation by the Japanese army, much remains of the indigenous, pre-Western Filipino society. A narration of the salient features of the Japanese invasion and the American occupation, as they appear to the villager, followed. The changing styles of clothing have been discussed. Houses — the tangible structures in which the individual eats, sleeps, takes care of his other physiological functions, rejoices, and despairs — have been described. The following chapter will deal with the socioeconomic composition of the village.

An old woman, age 65

Woman's work:
A typical wash day

An old-fashioned bamboo and nipa-thatched house

Women harvesting rice

3: Socioeconomic Structure

A FEW months previous to my entry into the village, a survey of village families had been completed by the elementary schoolteachers whose records were now ready for study. This survey, authorized by officials in the school system in 1953, was for the purpose of securing basic census data in regard to present and future school requirements. The teachers were told to list the heads of families, to visit each home, to record the number of individuals in each household, and to determine the number of these who were schoolchildren or preschool children. In 1954, additional items of information were ordered to be collected: presence and number of home gardens, fruit trees, pigs, chickens, and, in the interest of sanitary practices, latrines. When the teachers had gathered the data, the items were summarized and passed by the principal of the school to the Palo district supervisor, thence to the chief clerk at the division office in Tacloban, and finally to the central office in Manila.

The principal of the school generously made available to me the notebooks compiled by the teachers. Despite my initial doubts about the reliability of the data and a certain unevenness of collecting and recording from teacher to teacher, I received the material gratefully. The teachers had based their records in part on personal knowledge and in part on answers received in house-to-house questioning. One might harbor some doubts about the accuracy of their knowledge and question whether or not they sought, and persisted in seeking, the information about unknown items, or persevered in confirming the doubtful ones. Some of my misapprehension about the reliability of the source material was allayed when I learned that the school

23

officials had authorized a checking procedure on accuracy. For this purpose, nonvillage personnel had been hired. At randomly chosen houses, the checkers asked the survey questions once again and reviewed each entry made by the teacher. Thus the several reasons implicit in the above give confidence in the entries in the teachers' notebooks: the scope of the survey, the status of the officials authorizing it, and the procedure of using checkers.

I had the entries transferred from the teachers' notebooks to tally sheets. Two hundred sixty families had been listed in 1953-54. In January, 1956, when my assistants and I began our work, we had to make allowance for certain demographic changes. We found twenty-nine cases in which the family had moved away, or the household head had died, or the family had changed in some way so that it no longer existed in the same form as at the time of the teacher survey. We corrected the list and took the remaining 231 families as our baseline for study, not attempting to find or identify new families.

At this time, we were seeking basic economic data. In a house-to-house survey, we questioned members of the 231 families about (1) the amount and kind of land owned, (2) the use to which the land was put, (3) occupation of the family, (4) amount of monthly cash income, and (5) whether or not they owned their own home and the lot on which it was located. We did not use a structured interview but did have a check sheet for each household in order to ensure getting complete and comparable data.

Immediately it became apparent that we had to be concerned about the accuracy of reported estimates of land holdings. One procedure often used to obtain information about land holdings is to consult the property records. While such a procedure has certain undeniable advantages, it was inadvisable in this instance. First, I did not have the time nor the personnel necessary for such an extended endeavor. Second, there was reason to believe that individual and municipal property records were neither completely accurate nor up-to-date regarding actual land ownership. For example, while many land transactions are validated by a written document, a proportion are not so handled; in a minority of cases, only a verbal agreement is made. Even when property transactions are documented, the transaction may be spread over an extended time span and, in the process, the legal records will fail to reflect the changing ownership.

For instance, during the Japanese occupation a widow had borrowed money on a piece of land. In the years following the liberation she was unable to repay the loan and, in fact, increased the mortgage on the property. Fourteen years after the initial loan she was seeking a final loan, after which she promised to turn the land over to the moneylender. But still, at the time of the field work, the transaction was far from complete and the information about ownership which we obtained by talking to her and the moneylender was far more illuminating than that which could have been obtained from a review of the existing legal records. Therefore, we depended on personal interviews for our report. In addition to talking to land owners and moneylenders, we sometimes adopted the procedure of talking to more than one respondent about a household and thus we had a check on the accuracy of the initial report.

We also wanted to know something about the "occupation" of a given household. The establishment of an occupation also posed problems. That the Filipino does not work for prolonged, measured periods with single-minded attention to the task at hand is remarkable to the methodical clock-attuned Westerner. Village work patterns are much more casual; a man works unhurriedly, often laying aside the task, picking it up again, all the while carrying on spontaneous conversation and joking with his family, companions, or co-workers. But this easy manner does not mean that he is not industrious or that the work is shirked.

It may be worthwhile to widen our examination to work patterns of nonindustrial peoples in general. Herskovits has long since exploded the notion that preliterate people do as little work as they can. Abstracting from several ethnographies, Herskovits presents data showing that not only minimal, but considerable extra, energy is expended by nonliterate people in procuring their basic subsistence needs. Furthermore, they labor not only for their basic needs but also for any other given ends (securing magical paraphernalia or preparing a feast) as may be deemed necessary by cultural standards.[1]

In another interesting study involving quantitative techniques, Erasmus has further validated these observations. Over a period of three months, Erasmus and his wife recorded five thousand observations on two hundred villagers in Tenia, Mexico. The activity in which the villager was engaged when the researchers saw him comprised the content of each observation. The activities observed were divided into three classes: economic, household, and leisure. The economic classification included agriculture, fishing, hunting, tending cattle, making or repairing tools, etc.; household activities involved preparing and serving food, procuring water, cleaning clothes, and caring for children; leisure activities, lying down, sitting inactive, chatting, visiting, and so on.

Erasmus found, as might be expected, that household activities dominate the women's day and economic activities, the men's. He further found that the pattern of activity and leisure is related to the diurnal cycle and temperature changes. The villagers awakened and began their day's activities between dawn and sunrise. The women woke a little earlier than the men. During the cool hours of the morning the men worked wholeheartedly at economic pursuits. During the same hours the women were busy with household chores. As the midday heat increased, the labors decreased for both sexes. And, as the afternoon advanced, work was taken up again.[2]

This pattern also held true in Guinhangdan. In the morning I awakened to the sound of the cock's crow and the swishing of the rice baskets as the women began breakfast preparations. In the first wan light, a man could be seen going to the fields or the sea. By midmorning almost everyone was busy, but the midday siesta a few hours later was an almost inviolate custom. Economic and household activities resumed in midafternoon; dinner and leisure activities finished the day.

The work patterns of the Filipino are such that he can, and does, work competently but not hurriedly for irregular lengths of time on whatever task interests him at the moment. Then he may go on to something else, apparently forgetting the first job and often leaving it in a state of incompletion. How relevant to the establishment of an "occupation" is the amount of time spent on an activity and the patterning or lack of patterning of this time?

Another difficulty arose. Our earliest questioning revealed that no family was engaged in a single money-making or subsistence activity to the exclusion of all other activities and, furthermore, as has already been adumbrated, participation in any occupational activity was seldom systematized and regulated. In actuality, several activities ran serially or might have been undertaken simultaneously.[3] The socioeconomic situation in the village was such that a family which included a wage earner might also have a little rice patch. Very likely a copra grower would also do a little fishing. The wife of a laborer might have his salary and also do some sewing for cash. Two or more family members might contribute substantially to the maintenance of the household. Could we then, with any validity, designate a single occupation for each household?

We could and we did, and the key to the procedure is our definition of occupation. With the difficulties of formulation in mind, we decided to ask each household respondent about the *primary resources which were exploited for cash* in his household. The occupation is then defined as the exploiting of that resource, such as sewing nipa palm, fishing, laboring by contract, and so forth. Since almost all families have some such resource, the procedure worked out well. The definition adopted precluded the necessity of tying the occupation to a particular person. Instead, we spoke about the main occupation of an unspecified member of the household group. Such a procedure was justified in view of the close-knit quality of family life and the sharing and interchangeability of economic responsibility among the family members.

This approach provided two advantages. It yielded information about the resources that could be converted into cash to which any household had access, and it led into questions about income. A disadvantage of the system was that it did not tell what proportion of the household subsistence was cash-based. A household with little cash income might have a comfortable but not luxurious style of living which the occupation and income data might not indicate. A household whose subsistence activities were more attuned to a wage-and-market economy might have more cash but a less adequate food supply. Despite this shortcoming, we believed that if occupation were used as one of several basic items of information, we could use other items to verify, balance, or correct the impression of socioeconomic standing given.

Land ownership and occupation were two indices to socioeconomic standing. Money income was a third. We collected the information by asking for estimates of monthly income, a task which was not easy for the village people. They were accustomed to neither a clock nor a calendar. They did not think in terms of weeks; and a month was a significant interval only to a minority of salaried and pensioned people. Also, the villagers were not record oriented. Household records of expenditures and indebtedness were either nonexistent, or when they were kept they tended to be fragmentary and inconsistent. Despite the lack of written records and a lack of cultural prescription for record-keeping, we worked patiently with each family, using the partial records when they were available and making estimates on the past month's earnings when no record existed.

At each house we emphasized the need for frankness and candor in answering questions. The gathering of this kind of data almost always besets the researchers with difficulties and we were no exception. Occasionally the income figure reported to us was suspect because of the manner of the respondent in giving it. Sometimes it was incongruous in the light of what we knew of the family. I discussed the reliability of the data with my assistants who thought that most people were reporting honestly but that a small number might be less than completely candid for three reasons: (1) some might report an amount under their estimate for fear that their earnings might come to the attention of the Bureau of Internal Revenue whose collectors they had so far avoided or evaded; (2) some might report an amount under their estimate in the hope that succorant aid would be forthcoming from some benevolent source; (3) some might report an amount over their estimate in the hope of raising their prestige standing among the villagers who should hear of it.

In view of the questionable reliability of some of the monthly income figures, certain procedural checks were inaugurated. Each stated income was reviewed with regard to selected indicators to income, such as the type of house the family lived in, the presence and kind of furniture within it, amount and kind of entertaining undertaken, and the ownership of certain unusually expensive items such as livestock or a fish corral. All of these items require cash and cannot be obtained or accomplished without it. Furthermore, we privately collected information on moneylenders and debtors and reviewed this information against the stated incomes.

As a result of the review and the discrepancies noted, it was necessary to make upward revision in the income reported in eighteen cases where the standard of living of the family was at marked variance with the amount stated. Downward revision was thought necessary in one case but since the family was undoubtedly the wealthiest in the village and since the income reported, and that estimated by us, was in a category by itself, we did not change the figures.

We interviewed at least one member of every household in gathering basic economic data. In addition, a good deal of information was collected at this time through the traditional anthropological technique of interviewing knowledgeable informants about the subjects in which they were especially versed: land use, rental customs, systems of credit, tenancy procedures, etc. Their accounts were cross-checked with other respondents.

SOCIOECONOMIC DATA: PROCESSING

Some analysis of the data in the field was needed to have a preliminary idea of the existing socioeconomic levels. Normally the sorting, counting, and tabulation of information about 231 subjects is handled with the aid of punched cards and some device for searching and retrieving. We had neither punched cards nor mechanical aids of any sort and performed the processing operations by hand from the tally sheets, a tedious and onerous procedure not recommended to the reader.

Counts were made and cross-tabulations figured. The descriptive material from selected informants was checked for clarity and accuracy and transferred from notebooks to the card file.

SOCIOECONOMIC DATA: THE FINDINGS —
LAND OWNERSHIP

The 231 units referred to are *households* or units of residence. A household is here defined as a spatially enclosed unit wherein live a number of individuals usually related by birth or marriage. In instructions to census takers for the 1948 census in the Philippines, a household was defined by the operations designated. Thus, the primary criterion was that the members listed sleep in the house but a number of special cases must be considered. Servants who sleep in are listed as members of the household. Children who are living in a household other than that of their nuclear family because they are attending school at some distance from "home" are not counted as members of the household. People temporarily absent from the household because of internment in a hospital or prison are not counted as being in the household. Boarders or lodgers are counted where they sleep. Officers and enlisted men of the armed services are not counted in their home household.[4]

I followed most of these procedures in designating members of a household, except on two points. Schoolchildren residing in a household other than that of their nuclear family as members of the resident household were counted. Visitors in a household were included on the basis of the length of the visit since a visit might stretch out for months or be the beginning of a more permanent residence arrangement.

Table 1 shows the amount of land owned by various household groups. The land referred to in Table 1 is primarily field land, that is, level land at some distance from the home, whose actual or potential use is for the cultivation of crops. Almost all field land is to the south and west of the barrio; a few of the fields are farther south on the river and more difficult to reach. An insignificant amount of field land exists within the barrio and consists of narrow stretches along the river. None of the village field land is owned by absentee landlords. On the contrary, one Guinhangdan man owns a little land elsewhere in Leyte and one has some in Mindanao. In compiling the data for the table, land under mortgage was counted as belonging to the original owner. Land which had been inherited by a group and had not yet been divided was not counted, as this was an insignificant amount.

TABLE 1

LAND OWNERSHIP BY HOUSEHOLD GROUP

Amount of Land	Number of Holders	Percentage of Holders
No land	134	58
Less than a hectare	24	10
One to three hectares	52	23
Four to six hectares	12	5
Seven or more hectares	9	4
Totals	231	100%

The most significant factor revealed in Table 1 is that 134 households are without any field land whatsoever, or, conversely, all of the land is owned by people in 97 households. In percentages, this is 42 per cent owners and 58 per cent nonowners. The size of holdings ranged from a fraction of a hectare to two large tracts of seventeen and thirty hectares. Twenty-four families, or 10 per cent, had less than a hectare. Fifty-two households, or 23 per cent, had holdings of one to three hectares. Only twenty-one households, or 9 per cent, have four or more hectares.[5]

House and lot ownership may be considered separately from field ownership. It is remarkable that all but nine householders reported owning their own house. Renting is a system not present in the barrio and there appears to be little need for it, although it exists in the provincial capital. Although almost everybody owns his own home, the same is not true of lot ownership. Only a little over half of the village residents owns the lot on which their house is located (127 compared to 104).

LAND USE

Field land is used for growing rice, camotes, and other food crops. Coconuts are grown in symmetrical rows in groves and in less regular strips and patches; the nipa palm grows in marshy banks along the river. Banana and abaca trees are planted sporadically near houses. The few gardens are grown on house lots rather than in the fields which are suitable for crop cultivation. Fruit trees are located along the road and behind and beside houses.

TABLE 2

SIZE OF HOLDING AND LAND USE

Size of Holding	Use of Land	Number of Households
Less than a hectare	Works own land	10
	Works own land and has tenants or hires help	7
	Has tenants only	7
One to three hectares	Works own land and has tenants or hires help	30
	Has tenants only	18
Four to six hectares	Works own land and has tenants or hires help	4
	Has tenants only	8
Seven or more hectares	Has tenants only	8
	Total	92

Table 2 compares the size of holdings with the use made of the land, not in terms of crops planted but in terms of family labor, daily hired labor, and tenancy. Not counted in the table are 134 landless households and five households with holdings ranging from zero to nine hectares who for one reason or another did not cultivate their land the year the field work was done.

Since the size of a holding which can be worked by one family is limited, the owners of large tracts generally hire tenants to work the land for them. Owners of any size holding may have a tenant but, significantly, no tract of more than a hectare is worked by the owners alone. This suggests that a holding larger than a hectare is either difficult, impossible, or unprofitable to farm without hired labor or tenants. Note, too, that the eight households with tracts of more than seven hectares have tenants only, do none of their own farming, and do not use day labor. Apparently, the larger the size of the holdings, the less likely is the owner to do his own farming. Also, as his holdings become substantial, he is more apt to exchange a system of daily or seasonal labor for one of tenancy.

Some description of tenancy arrangement is in order. Tenancy arrangements are usually verbal and most commonly involve the exchange of the tenant's labor for one half of the crop yield. (A less common arrangement gives two-thirds of the crop to the tenant who must then pay all expenses.) The landowner seeks the tenant, preferring a man with a reputation for honesty and industry. The tenant, on his part, prefers an owner with a reputation for generosity and lenience. In local terms, this means a man who not only provides for a fair division of the crops but who will also agree to feed the harvesters (usually relatives of the tenant) with rice at harvest time.

When a landowner has a prospective tenant in mind, he may send a note or visit him to discuss the matter. The prospective tenant asks about the terms of the agreement. These may include the right to build a house on the land or to occupy one that is already there. The owner enumerates the responsibilities: tenant is to clear the fields, plant, and harvest. Sometimes, when the land has lain fallow for several years and is heavily overgrown, additional men are hired to clear the land. The tenant and the owner estimate the cost of paying and feeding the helpers and share the costs half and half. It may also be the tenant's responsibility and expense to fence the land if deemed advisable. Further subsidiary agreements between the two may involve carabao or coconuts. The owner supplies carabao (water buffalo) and the tenant cares for them, with the privilege of using them for nonfarming chores. If some of the land being cultivated is already planted in coconuts, both the owner and the tenant gather and share the nuts.

Clearing, planting, and harvesting are the periods of heaviest work for a farmer. No fertilizer is used, no weeding is done, and while irrigation is not common, a ditch is sometimes dug to a water source. The owner and the tenant visit each other infrequently during the course of the crop growth. When the crops are harvested and ready for division, owner and tenant are both present for the transaction. Following that all-important formality, their relationship as tenant and owner continues without further discussion or contract unless the tenant has displeased the owner.

OCCUPATIONS

One of the reasons Guinhangdan had been chosen for study was its character as an agricultural-fishing village. The study of such a village would offer insight into the way of life of both fishermen and farmers. I had expected a high degree of homogeneity of occupation from preliminary description, and was not prepared for the variety of occupations we found when we began our investigation. In the categorization of occupations that follows, many of the terms are self-descriptive, but some require explanation. The difference between a *fisherman* and a *fish vendor*, for instance, is attributable to the rise of middlemen in various occupations in the Philippines in recent decades. Thus, at one time the same man who caught the fish took them to market, but today increasingly more often vendors go to the shore, buy the catch from the fisherman, and take them to market in large lots. As might be expected in a village with the location and environment of Guinhangdan, fishermen are the largest single occupational group, but as might not be expected, in fifteen households fish vending was the main occupation whereas fishing was the chief activity in only thirty-seven.

The next largest group of workers I have termed the laborers. By definition, laborers lack any resource except their physical strength. They are hired by the day or for the duration of a specific job and are most commonly found clearing land, aiding in house building (where they must be differentiated from the skilled and better-paid carpenters), or husking coconuts. Their pay is low and their days of unemployment are many. In thirty households, a male's hired labor was the principal source of money income.

The third largest occupational group were the nipa palm-thatch weavers. Gathering and preparing of thatches for roofing was the main source of cash for twenty-two households.

Farmers comprise the next two groups: twenty families who have no coconut trees and are primarily rice growers, and nineteen farmers whose main crop is copra. Here, too, the numbers are somewhat smaller than expected.

According to some definitions the next occupation, *pensioned*, is not an occupation, but under the terms of our definition it is. Twelve households receive their main source of money income from the pension paid by the government to one of its members.

Ropemakers, those who owned and processed the fiber of abaca trees, also numbered twelve. In nine households, the main source of

TABLE 3

FREQUENCY DISTRIBUTION OF OCCUPATIONS

Occupation	Number of Households
Fisherman	37
Laborer	30
Palm-thatch weaver	22
Farmer (excluding copra)	20
Copra grower and dryer	19
Fish vendor	15
Pension receiver	12
Ropemaker	12
Supported by children	9
Carpenter	9
Small store owner	7
Clerk	6
Teacher	5
Palm-wine gatherer	3
Policeman	3
Seamstress	3
Fish-basket maker	2
Firewood seller	2
Bus or jeep driver	2
Mechanic	2
Lawyer	1
Curer (native)	1
Clam seller	1
Jeep owner	1
Palm-thatch vendor	1
Palm-wine seller	1
Dealer in used clothing	1
Leaf tobacco seller	1
Carabao husbandry	1
Maid	1
Laundress	1
Total	231

cash consisted of contributions from the children both in and away from the household. In another nine households, carpentry was the main occupation. Seven families received money income through ownership of a small store.

Six households received their cash income from members who were clerical workers, usually in the government employ since private industry is so little developed. An elementary schoolteacher member was the primary source of money income for five families.

Table 3 shows the kinds and frequency distribution of all occupations reported. In the interests of economy and because they are not numerically important, the remaining occupations will not be discussed.

CASH INCOME

When the individual household incomes were listed, the incomes reported ranged from no cash at all to a dependable P650.00 a month. (P stands for *peso*. At the time of fieldwork, two pesos equaled one American dollar.) While this is a wide range, the distribution of income among the 231 families is not equal along the range. For ease in reading and analyzing, the income figures have been collapsed to six categories (see Table 4).

TABLE 4

DISTRIBUTION OF CASH INCOME

Income per month (in pesos)	Number of Households
0 to 15	34
16 to 30	106
31 to 60	43
61 to 105	17
106 to 150	10
151 and above	21
Total	231

Table 4 shows that thirty-four families manage to exist with no cash at all or with as little as fifteen pesos a month. The members of these thirty-four households are of interest. Apparently, some individuals still live wholly on a subsistence (noncash) basis. Also in this category are some people who undoubtedly are more dependent on their own unsalaried efforts and who participate less in the money economy than do others. Some of the households in this category include old couples who are childless or whose children have left home. The needs of the elderly are modest and their tolerance of deprivation is spartan. Finally, in this category of extremely low cash incomes we find families who exist only by incurring greater and greater debts for daily or ceremonial needs.

Nearly half the village families cluster in the next category — P16 to P30 — the restricted income on which 106 of 231 families live. The figures are a telling index to the compelling poverty of the simple peasant. The 140 families whose income is below thirty pesos a month are highly dependent on aid and credit from their fellow villagers.

A substantial number of families — forty-three — have a cash income of P31 to P60. Only forty-eight families earn more than P61 a month. It is in this group that we find the moneylenders. A description of the credit systems that make living with little cash possible is in order. Casual, constant indebtedness, in monetary and other terms, is a way of life in the village, not an isolated condition.

The practice of mortgaging land is a credit system that has already been mentioned. Mortgaging of land is not undertaken lightly. It is generally a last resort and one which the owner undertakes with reluctance. Sometimes mortgages can be repaid but more often the borrower eventually loses the land, undoubtedly the story of many of the 134 landless people. The fact that half the harvest of mortgaged land goes to the moneylender adds to the difficulties of repayment of the borrower.

Two other procedures to raise cash are *pataya* and *palangoy*. Pataya refers to the loan of money on a potential coconut crop. An owner of coconut trees, in need of money before the nuts are ripe, makes a verbal agreement with a wealthy villager. In exchange for cash, the tree owner promises unhusked nuts to be delivered to the moneylender. In 1956 the prevailing rate of exchange was one hundred nuts for P5. Palangoy is a similar transaction in which money is loaned on the collateral of a rice crop. The crop-raiser borrows a set amount which is returned in rice at harvest time, the amount of rice depending on the market price in the village and the town. There are no interest charges on the mortgage of a crop.

Small shacklike stores with a very restricted line of produce are numerous in the village. These stores extend credit and almost everyone within the radius of their operation buys on credit. The customers' debts, *otang*, may be trifling (five centavos for the purchase of lard) or they may be considerable as they accumulate over a long period of time. (Two centavos equaled one American penny.) The relationship between a creditor and a debtor of no fixed income is one of indebtedness on the part of the debtor and long-term, noninterest-bearing credit on the part of the creditor. There is no Waray Waray word for this understanding.

A different relationship exists between a creditor and a debtor of established credit and fixed income. In the first instance, the debtor is unemployed or has a low, sporadic income. In the second instance, the debtor has an income, probably monthly, and holds a status occupation. When such a desirable customer and a proprietor do business together they enter into an arrangement called *suki*; it is said that they become suki to each other. The debtor is obliged to purchase from the owner all the materials he needs which the owner carries. The owner is obligated to supply the debtor and to keep his credit extended. Written accounts of indebtedness are kept. The debtor may pay part, or all, of his bill on his payday but the two continue in their arrangement indefinitely.

LAND OWNERSHIP AND OCCUPATIONS

One of the first factors to be investigated was whether a relationship existed between land ownership and occupation. Do the landed people tend to be the farmers? Do the people without land cluster in certain occupational groups? Are all occupations represented both among those with and without land? A study of Table 5 throws some light on these questions. Only the landless are considered.

Fishermen and laborers comprise the largest group of nonland owners. Fish vendors, ropemakers, palm-thatch weavers, and people supported by their children are next. Carpenters, small store owners, pension receivers, and tenant farmers complete the listing. All other occupations are represented by a single household or not at all. The occupational distribution of landed people is seen in Table 6.

Among the landowners, farming is the most common occupation, palm-thatch weaving next, and the third largest group receive pensions. After that, the numbers become insignificant. In summary, we have only three occupational groups of substantial size: the landless fishermen, laborers, and the land-owning farmers. The only excep-

TABLE 5

OCCUPATIONS OF LANDLESS HOUSEHOLDS

Occupation	Number of Households
Fisherman	33
Laborer	27
Fish vendor	11
Ropemaker	9
Palm-thatch weaver	8
Supported by children	7
Carpenter	6
Small store owner	4

Tenant farmers:
    copra (3)
    without copra (1)
	4

Pension receiver	3
All other occupations	22
Total	134

TABLE 6

OCCUPATIONS OF LANDOWNERS

Occupation	Number of Households
Farmer: copra (16) without copra (19)	35
Palm-thatch weaver	14
Pension receiver	9
Clerks	5
Teachers	4
Fish vendors	4
Fishermen	4
Carpenter	3
Small store owner	3
Ropemaker	3
Laborer	3
Supported by children	2
All other occupations	8
Total	97

tions to these relations between land ownership and occupation are four families with land who reported fishing as their main occupation and three landed families who reported laboring as their main money income.

From the data collected on land use and from talks with village elders, it became apparent that tenancy was widespread. Yet in the data on occupations only four households reported tenant farming as their main occupation. This anomaly occurs because these data are collected from village dwellers only. The tenant families who did not have homes in the village but lived out on the farms (and this includes most of them) are not counted.

LAND OWNERSHIP AND INCOME

An examination of the incomes in relation to land ownership did not yield a clear picture. However, 105 households with no land had incomes in the zero- to thirty-peso range and 30 households with one hectare or more land were in the range of sixty-one pesos and above. Thus, some relationship does appear to exist between land ownership per se and the amount of cash in a household, but the relationship is complicated by many factors: location and fertility of land, size of holdings, use made of land, labor arrangements, probably individual business acumen, age of the landholders, size of the family, and so forth.

OCCUPATION AND INCOME

Table 7 represents the findings on the relationship of occupation to income. The table shows that the consistently highest-paid peo-

TABLE 7

OCCUPATION AND INCOME

OCCUPATION	RANGE OF INCOME IN PESOS			
	0 to 15	16 to 30	31 to 60	61 and above
Clerk	0	0	0	6
Teacher	0	0	0	5
Pension receiver	1	1	2	8
Small store owner	0	1	2	3
Carpenter	1	2	3	3
Farmers:				
with copra (19)	0	14	16	9
without copra (20)				
Fish vendor	1	9	3	2
Ropemaker	4	7	1	0
Laborer	1	24	3	2
Fisherman	3	27	6	1
Palm-thatch weaver	8	11	2	1
Supported by children	9	0	0	0
All others	6	10	5	8
Totals	34	106	43	48

ple are the clerks, teachers, and the pensioned. Next in order come the small store owners and the carpenters. Farmers are found in the three upper ranges of income; none earns below fifteen pesos a month. The people with the least money income are those supported by children, the palm-thatch weavers, fishermen, laborers, and rope-makers. Fish vendors are found in all ranges of income but predominate in the lower half of the range.

STRATIFICATION

When I first began living in the village, I thought that there were no social classes, that is, no great differences in the way of life as it affected housing, food, clothing, and opportunities. A dead monotony seemed to permeate a material culture which did not include the subtleties that surround the variations in possessions and habits from class to class found elsewhere. However, greater familiarity with the society changed this point of view. There *were* differences in housing, diet, and clothing as well as in more intangible aspects. The tourist's easy dismissal of the "bamboo shacks" in which the villagers live overlooks slight differences which become substantial when one lives with them. A one-room thatched roof house which is basically unfurnished affords different life experiences than that of a house with several rooms, galvanized iron roof, and a good deal of furniture.

A meager diet which includes corn more often than rice and includes little else may be contrasted with the fuller, diversified menu of the more prosperous. A single outfit of worn clothing may be contrasted with the several costumes and different styles of those who are well-to-do. More important than any of these material aspects, however, are the differentials in prestige and esteem given individuals according to their rank. And, as elsewhere in the world, responsibility and privilege differ from rank to rank.

Once differences in the lifeways of the people became apparent, it became desirable to study the magnitude of those differences. No less importantly, it became desirable to seek a clarification of the local manifestation of social class. Very little investigation had been made of social classes in the Philippines although much had been written about social stratification in America, the major portion of the work being done by sociologists. The study of stratification is based on the fact that members of a society classify each other into categories and rank these categories. People are accredited or discredited according to certain social and personal characteristics. One category is considered superior to another concerning certain qualifications which may or may not be made specific. The delineation of the classes or strata and of the criteria on which the ranking is based presents one of the main problems in the study of stratification.

A careful review of the published data on social stratification will reveal that all studies may be categorized as evidencing one of three main approaches: subjective, reputational, and objective.[6] In the subjective approach, the respondents in the study are asked where they place themselves in the ranking system. On the basis of these answers, the investigator then describes the subjective strata in that particular society. In the reputational approach, the respondents are asked to place other people in the categories in which they perceive them. Even where classes are not perceived as such, individuals are well aware of the system of ranking and may, if they are otherwise articulate, speak of the place of any given individual in relationship to other individuals. The investigator can then describe the reputational strata of the society. In the objective approach, the investigator decides what criteria are used in determining the strata, what the strata are, and who is in each.

As is explicit from this chapter, I have used the objective approach. The criteria to class affiliation in Guinhangdan are land ownership, occupation, and income.[7] Two recent studies confirm the relevance of these criteria to the system of stratification in the Philippine area. In the Lynch study on a Bikol town, the investigator used a reputational approach to stratification. He asked his respondents to assign their fellow community members to categories of their own specification, and found that they depended heavily on economic criteria. Of fifty-two criteria employed by the townspeople, twenty-five were economic; twelve, political; and fifteen, personal. Furthermore, he found that *ownership of land* and *possession of money* were the two most frequently mentioned economic indicators.[8] Later, he studied the actual land ownership patterns and the money incomes to see if these did indeed point to class membership. Not unexpectedly he found that monied people who owned land were referred to as the "big people." The rest of the townspeople were frequently referred to in conversation by the stereotype, "little people."[9]

In another study, an attempt was made to determine whether

Filipinos evaluated occupations in a manner similar to the evaluations made in America and elsewhere. The investigator chose as his units of investigation five barrios near Manila.[10] He found that occupations are evaluated to a very high degree much the way that they are in industrialized and/or Western countries. Certain occupations tend to be ranked as higher in prestige and value than others and, in consequence, the practitioners of certain occupations enjoy a higher prestige.

The findings of both these studies have relevance to this one. Although a certain caution is necessary in applying the findings to the Guinhangdan material, because of the differences of the units of comparison, both the Lynch and the Tirykian studies confirm the choice of criteria to social class. Once the existence of classes is determined and the principal criteria established, it is customary to ascertain the number of classes within the society. Such classification is arbitrary with each investigator and the number of classes discerned has ranged from two to six. The same data may be interpreted differently by different investigators, presenting variant pictures of the class structure. Lynch characterizes the Bikol town as having two classes, whereas Tirykian is not concerned with social classes.

For my part, I am aware that when we come to divide the society into classes, the same problems that we faced when we chose criteria to rank people arise again. A decision has to be made concerning the relevance, practicality, and fruitfulness of criteria to any cutting point established. I knew the people of the Philippines to be in large part a two-class society, but recent history of the Philippines and in many comparable areas had shown that there was a slowly emerging middle class. My experience in the village verified the existence of that emerging middle.

Next, two questions had to be faced: How should a middle class in general be characterized and how should it be identified within the village? I characterized a middle class in general as occurring only in societies with a high degree of specialization of labor, both internal and external trade, established markets, and a money economy. All are found to some degree both in the village and throughout the Philippines. Another characteristic of classes is that the members have patterns of production, distribution, and consumption which differ from class to class. While the data presented in this chapter contain nothing on consumption patterns, and only mention dis-

tribution indirectly, the material is much fuller on matters of production. A review of land ownership, occupation, and income may
reveal a number of classes. Are there any groups which consistently
have less prestigious occupations and less money? Conversely, are
there any groups which consistently have more prestigious occupations and more money?

Some groups have, as it were, a ceiling on their earnings and their
income does not often exceed a rather low amount. Thus, of nine
households supported by children, none has an income higher than
fifteen pesos. These are definitely in the lowest class as far as opportunity and way of life are concerned. Thus, of seventy-nine fishermen, laborers, and ropemakers, sixty-six earn less than thirty-one
pesos a month and only three earn more than sixty pesos. Most of
these, too, are definitely in the lower class. Of twenty-three palm-
thatch weavers, nineteen earn less than thirty-one pesos a month. A
study of the land ownership of these four occupational groups con-
firms the picture. Thirty-three fishermen own no land; four do.
Twenty-seven laborers own no land; three do. Of twelve ropemakers,
nine do not own any land. Of the nine supported by children only
two have a small patch of land. Fourteen palm-thatch weavers own
land but most of this consists of small strips of land on which the
palm is grown.

If some groups have a ceiling on their earnings, others have a
floor; they do not earn less than a certain amount. Thus clerks and
teachers are in a class by themselves. None earns less than sixty-one
pesos a month. Pension receivers are on the high earning end of the
scale, too. In these three groups (clerks, teachers, and pension receivers) of twenty-three individuals only one does not own land
and this family is aberrant in not wanting to own any land.

Practitioners of other occupations span the scale of income range.
Arbitrarily I am placing these, whose earnings, occupation, and income do not show clear-cut placement either high or low, in the
middle class. This is a different meaning for "middle class" from that
assumed in well-developed industrial societies, but we are not deal-
ing with a well-developed industrial society. Also, what I term as
"middle class" in the village may be quite differently characterized
as it is studied in Philippine towns or cities. The differences between
the "middle class" in these larger units and the "middle class" in
Guinhangdan may be greater than the differences between the "middle" and "lower" classes in Guinhangdan.

In American society, clerks and teachers are middle class; pension receivers are generally among the poorest and most pitied. But in Philippine society, where money is scarce and the earning level of the whole country remarkably low, teachers, clerks and pensioners, more often than not, form the elite of the village. This system of reckoning places farmers and carpenters in the middle class along with the lawyer, mechanic, jeep driver, and native curer.

On the whole, the framework is a bit gross and does not fit perfectly, but it does act as a reliable indicator to substantial differences in life opportunities and patterns of production and consumption.

In summary, I have made an effort to delineate the gross economic factors which have pervasive and overriding effects on the lifeways of individuals and families. To do this, land ownership, land use, occupation, and cash income were considered. Some of the difficulties of establishing land ownership, of specifying occupation, and of recording income were outlined. Finally, on the basis of the data thus gathered and on inferences made in consequence of them, a strata system of three levels was postulated. We now turn our attention from the macro-unit, the village, to one of the micro-units within it, the household.

4: Household Composition

HOUSEHOLD census sheets provide the data on which this section is based. A procedure for establishing who is a member of a given household has already been discussed. (See Chapter 3, "Socioeconomic Data: The Findings — Land Ownership.") A household is further defined as a spatially enclosed unit in which a number of individuals live who are usually related by birth or marriage. Minimally, a household involves a specialization of area for food preparation; functionally speaking, a household group is a commensal and coresiding group. The privileges and responsibilities of one member to another are decided by their family relationships rather than by the fact that they reside together. The composition of the families inhabiting the 129 households is a complex matter and will constitute the principal material in this chapter.

A household census sheet contains these items of information: (1) the name of the household head as indicated by the respondent, (2) the names of every other individual in the household, (3) the occupation of the household head and that of any other major producer in the household, (4) the relationship of every individual in the house to the household head, and for each individual, (5) age, (6) birth date, and (7) education.

Household census data were collected over the entire period of the field stay, but not for every household. The procedure was to collect this information from a respondent before beginning an extended interview. Many households were visited to collect data with which to build rapport, widen contacts, extend general knowledge, and include people in the household census who were not otherwise

45

Name	Age	Occupation and Relationship	Birth Date	Education
Jose Mora	36	Farmer	DK	5th Grade
Edita Mora	35	Wife	11/21/21	6th Grade
Jose Mora, Jr.	16	Son	2/5/40	1st Yr. High
Luz Mora	14	Daughter	7/29/42	6th Grade
Angel Mora	11	Daughter	8/16/43	3rd Grade
Generosa Mora	9	Daughter	2/23/47	1st Grade
Leopoldo Mora	7	Son	3/10/49	not in school
Filemon Mora	4	Son	5/6/52	not in school

Fig. 3. Household census sheet.

respondents. Thus census data were recorded in the process of a stroll and a chat, an informal visit, or an arranged interview. I recorded the data in pencil and, on return to my residence, transferred it to typewritten five-by-eight-inch sheets. Of a total of 231 households, census data were secured on 129, or better than half the total households listed. From the information recorded on the face side of a census sheet, a kinship chart was drawn on the reverse side. Thus:

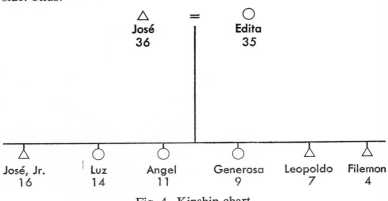

Fig. 4. Kinship chart.

Nonkin resident in the household were also included in the census with information as to their derivation and presence, for example, adopted child or a servant, a visitor, etc.

The reliability of the information in the household census is based on the care that is exercised in collecting and recording it. In the course of census taking, several sources of error were revealed and safeguards were devised to guard against them. For instance, in the listing of names we found that old women or prominent local women were often called by their maiden names. This is a reflection of the matronymic system of the old society which is in state of transition to patronymic. It is inevitable that societies are in a process of change while being studied, but the anthropologist's records based on the society either must have some unchanging system of designation or constitute a detailed study documenting the transition. We chose an unchanging system of designation, using patronymic naming because that is the direction of the present trend as well as the practice of the majority of the people.

Patronymic naming is traceable to the fact that public and church officials under both Spanish and American rule recognized a male head of the house and that the present civil code requires a woman to use her husband's name. Still, the change from matronymic naming is not complete, and a female will not always report her married name when identifying herself. Frequent checks were necessary to be sure that we were recording the married name as well as maiden surname.

Difficulties in designating occupations are discussed elsewhere.[1]

Information about the relationships of individuals within a household was easily obtained and unquestionably reliable. The collecting of age data was slow, uncertain, and beset with difficulties. Proffered figures were often based on guesses which we did our best to refine. Whenever possible we would secure the actual birth date, and the birth certificate was brought from the storage chest many times for this purpose. No birth certificates exist for the older people, and, accordingly, the record is less reliable. The record of education may be used with confidence; we questioned in terms of grades completed and have no reason to believe the answers to be anything but honest and unbiased.

HOUSEHOLD DATA-PROCESSING

For analysis it was deemed advisable to sort the households into types by family composition. The criteria for deriving types were sought in the families themselves. As a point of departure, I looked for a pair of spouses of reproductive age, or what might be called a procreating pair. A procreating pair is defined as a husband and wife with the wife between the ages of fifteen and thirty-five; the age of the male not considered.

Since at this time I was concerned with the social environment in the home of a particular child, I was further interested in whether or not a given pair of spouses were the biological as well as social parents of the children in that household. It is logical that if an adult not the biological parent enters the home, a different social environment is created from that in which the two parents have been the child's socializer since he was born. Such discrimination yielded two types of nuclear households. Of course, in those households where one parent was missing, the environment of the child and his consequent experiences again were different. This created another type of household.

The question now became how to classify a household when there were members in it other than the nuclear family. I envisioned this as extension on two dimensions, vertically and horizontally. If the extra member were a sibling of either parent, I thought of this as a horizontal extension. If the extra member were a grandparent or someone in the grandparental generation, I considered this as vertical extension. The presence of any of these members might be important for the kinds of activity that would prevail in that household. After a few days of sorting, the following categories appeared most practical and meaningful for further analysis.

I *Intact Nuclear.* An intact nuclear family is one in which married or common-law spouses live with their own or adopted children in a household; no other kin are present in the household. (See Fig. 4 for schematic representation of Intact Nuclear Family.)

II *Truncated Nuclear.* A truncated nuclear family is one in which one of the spouses is dead, divorced, or has deserted or separated, or, for some other cause (extreme illness, extended periods of labor on another island) is not part of the household. The family has not been reconstructed or re-established, that is, no remarriage has taken place or any other rearrangement been made.

III *Re-established Nuclear.* A re-established nuclear family is what its name suggests. The family had been broken by some form of separation, destruction, or loss and then re-established by a remarriage, a new marriage, or some other arrangement.

IV *Extended Horizontal.* An extended horizontal family is one in which a sibling of either the husband or wife live in the household (see Fig. 5).

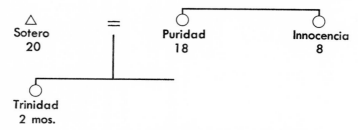

Fig. 5. Extended horizontal family type.

V *Extended Vertical.* An extended vertical family is one which is extended by the presence of three or four generations in the household. It may or may not include siblings of the husband or wife (see Fig. 6).

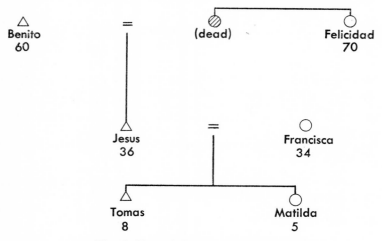

Fig. 6. Extended vertical family type.

VI *Skipped Generation Extended Vertical.* A skipped generation extended vertical family is one which is composed of an elderly person or persons (who are generally grandparents) and one or more of their own, their siblings', or someone else's grandchildren (see Fig. 7).

VII *Truncated or Residual.* A truncated or residual family is one in which there is but one or two members in the household and they are old or elderly.

VIII *Idiosyncratic.* The idiosyncratic families resisted classification. Here are four of them.

    a. A married, separated woman sharing a residence with her brother.

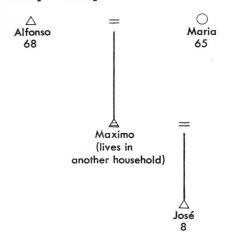

Fig. 7. Skipped generation extended
vertical type.

No children had resulted from her marriage but she had three of her own children in the household, each the child of a different man.

b. A young man married to a woman twice his age. The couple were childless but he had two children by other women, one in the village and one elsewhere.

c. Two large families temporarily sharing a residence while the house of one was being built.

d. An elderly couple aged forty-five and fifty-one with a five-year-old son of their own, a thirteen-year-old son of the wife by a former husband and two of the wife's cousins, aged fourteen and twenty-two.

HOUSEHOLD DATA FINDINGS: INTACT NUCLEAR FAMILIES

Fifty-nine intact nuclear families were present in the 129 households investigated. The fifty-nine intact nuclear families included four families with five adopted children among them and two families in which a spouse of a young married child was living in the house. Where young married children are found in the intact nuclear family, they have no children of their own. There are, thus, only two generations in the household.

The frequency age distribution of parents in intact nuclear families is shown in Table 8. No parent is under twenty years of age. It is somewhat of a surprise as well as a reflection of the age at which young folk marry that no father is under twenty-five and only four mothers are. On the other hand, only one mother is over fifty-five but seven fathers are. Most of the parents are between the ages of twenty-five and fifty-four.

In most cases the husband is older than the wife, but there are five cases where the wife is older by one to twenty years. Table 9 shows the comparative ages of husbands and wives.

TABLE 8

FREQUENCY AGE DISTRIBUTION OF PARENTS
IN INTACT NUCLEAR FAMILIES

Age	Father	Mother
20 to 24	0	4
25 to 34	13	15
35 to 44	25	26
45 to 54	14	13
55 to 64	2	1
65 and over	5	0
Totals	59	59

TABLE 9

COMPARATIVE AGES OF HUSBAND AND WIFE

Comparative Ages	Number of Cases
Spouses are same age	5
Wife is older than husband	5
Husband is older by:	
1 year	7
2 years	5
3 years	6
4 years	9
5 years	3
6–10 years	11
11–15 years	3
16–20 years	3
21 and more years	2
Total	59

The frequency age distribution of children in intact nuclear families is interesting. Seventy-one males out of 123 and 57 females out of 115 are in the zero to nine range. Eleven boys and eleven girls are over twenty, supporting the previous findings and suggesting that

TABLE 10

FREQUENCY AGE DISTRIBUTION OF CHILDREN
IN INTACT NUCLEAR FAMILIES

Age	Males	Females
0 to 4	33	28
5 to 9	38	29
10 to 14	22	32
15 to 19	19	15
20 to 24	8	9
25 to 29	3	2
Totals	123	115

marriages are not common before twenty years of age. Table 10 presents the frequency age distribution of children in intact nuclear families.

The size and range of an intact nuclear family is of interest. Table 11 includes both parents and children in the counts. To arrive at the number of children in each family, subtract two parents.

TABLE 11

SIZE OF INTACT NUCLEAR FAMILIES

Number of Persons in Family	Number of Cases
Three	9
Four	12
Five	12
Six	13
Seven	8
Eight	8
Nine	7
Ten	4
Eleven	4
Total	59

In gathering the figures on the size of family range, no listing was made of dead children, either those stillborn or those who died in infancy and childhood. In addition, a few families have another child or two than is listed here; such a child might be living in another household, away on an extended visit or working in another village, town, or city. Occasionally a married child has left the household, but this is rare because of comparative youth of the parents. The figures on size of family, then, refer to individuals present in the household. The range of family size is three to eleven members. The mode is six; the mean is eight and one-half and the median is six. The range of the number of children in intact nuclear families is one to nine. The mode is four; the mean is six and one-half and the median is four.

Intact nuclear families include all socioeconomic levels and a wide range of occupations. The size of their houses range from one-room shacks to substantial six-room, two-level structures, but the majority are not of the upper level nor do they possess the more substantial material possessions because of the comparative youth of the parents. Especially is this apt to be true if there are many children in the family. While children are desired and welcomed, for some they are recognized as an economic burden. On the other hand, a nuclear family with few children and industrious members is apt to be financially well off. But the general feeling is that many children are desirable because they can help one another throughout their lives.

TRUNCATED NUCLEAR

There were nine truncated nuclear families in our sample. No divorced people live in the village; there is a legal as well as a religious prohibition of divorce. In the entire village there was one case of separation, a husband who had left his wife and gone to another village. No cases of desertion were reported. Eight of the truncated nuclear families were cases of the loss of one spouse through death. It is interesting to note how an "orphan" is defined in this society. In our society, the usage is that a child who has lost both parents is an orphan. In Guinhangdan a child becomes an orphan on the death of a mother alone. If the father dies, the child is considered "unlucky" or bereaved but not orphaned. If the mother dies, the child will be given to a female relative of either parent to be reared unless he has female siblings old enough to take an active part in raising him. The ninth case was a family in which the husband had been working in Mindanao for seven months and planned to stay on for an indeterminate time.

One of the households is composed of a father aged seventy and a daughter aged thirty-eight. The child was eight when her mother died and the girl never married, nor did the father remarry.

The number of children in truncated nuclear families range from one to four. In one household a married daughter's spouse is resident; the daughter and her husband have no children. The single parent in each household ranges in age from thirty to seventy. Only two own any land and most are in the lowest socioeconomic level.

RE-ESTABLISHED NUCLEAR

There were four re-established nuclear cases. Two of the cases represented a remarriage of a surviving spouse. The third and fourth were rather unusual. An unwed mother whose child's father had never been resident in the village was married by a village man. The village man had previously been married to a woman in her family (one wife was the daughter of the third cousin of the other) who had died and he wanted to retain the family affiliation which boasted a brother-in-law in Manila who provided wide opportunities to place relatives in good jobs. The husband had a thirteen-year-old child of his own, treated both children equally well, and at the time of the writing, the wife's child was being put through college. The fourth case was similar. A father with two children of his own married an unwed mother. They now have a child of their own, bringing the total number of children in the household to four; they are among the poor.

EXTENDED HORIZONTAL

Five extended horizontal families included two cases in which the sibling was the husband's brother; two, the wife's sister; and one, the husband's sister. The cases are too few and the siblings too varied to generalize about the sibling most likely to be found in a household. Need rather than the particular kin relationship appears to determine the move when a sibling joins the household. The need may be mutual — for example, the household may welcome another pair of hands. Two of the households were large, with seven and eight children, respectively. The sibling who comes in (or stays in) may be older or younger. One was a child of eight; two were in their twenties, and two were over sixty. In one case of a well-to-do family, the husband's brother who was resident was attending normal school in the nearby town; presumably a temporary arrangement of several years. In no case did the sibling who joined the household have a spouse or bring a child with them.

EXTENDED VERTICAL

Among thirty-five cases of extended vertical families, only four had representatives from four generations; thirty-one were composed of members of three generations. As might be expected, some of these households number many members but, as might not be expected, some do not. One has three members, four have four, five have five, and eight have six. Of the remainder of the households, four have seven members, six have eight, five have nine, and one each have ten and eleven (see Table 12).

TABLE 12

FREQUENCY DISTRIBUTION OF NUMBER OF PERSONS
IN EXTENDED VERTICAL FAMILIES

Number of Persons in Family	Number of Cases
Three	1
Four	4
Five	5
Six	8
Seven	4
Eight	6
Nine	5
Ten	1
Eleven	1
Total	35

The household listed with eleven persons includes two unrelated members, a girl of thirteen and a boy of sixteen who are servants. The family is reputed and reported to be the wealthiest in the village and is singular, not in having a servant, but in having two servants and in calling them servants. A few of the larger prosperous families have a servant, but more often a child or two is adopted from a relative, or a poor family, and to these unfortunates fall the drudgery of which the natural children have less.

The situation with adopted children in extended families differs from that of adopted children in nuclear families. In nuclear families, the child is treated similarly to the natural children, but in the larger extended family, perhaps because of the added work inherent in feeding and housing a larger group, the adopted child is apt to be treated in a discriminatory fashion. Socioeconomic status also enters the picture. Several of the extended vertical families are both the most wealthy and the most upwardly striving. The kinds of activity that validate wealth and that raise social status call for many workers as well as material resources. An adopted daughter or two can be a definite advantage at times of feasts and in serving visitors. Also, adopted boys of teen age can be sent out to watch over lands planted but not yet harvested, thus saving the crop which might have had to be shared with a tenant. In the village as a whole, more often than not, the adopted child is a relative; probably the treatment of the child also varies with the degree of relatedness. Although there are too few cases for a generalization, adopted children do seem to get as much education as the other children in the family. No papers are needed in adoption. It is accomplished through verbal agreement of the adults involved but, in at least one case, a six-year-old boy was adopted into his grandparental household because he preferred it to his parents' home. Children adopted at the death of a mother have already been mentioned.

Taking each household as a unit containing three or four levels of individuals, the great-grandparental, the grandparental, the parental, and the children, how many individuals are on each level? When generation lines are not clear (as they were not in one instance), those over fifty years of age are assigned to the grandparental, twenty to fifty to the parental, and under twenty years, to the children.

From Table 13 it can be noted that the presence of only four great-grandparents (one each in four households out of 129 households) attests to the relative lack of longevity in the village. While we lack rates for actual morbidity and age at death, this finding is a clear indication of the rarity of individuals who live a long life. Of the four great-grandparents, two were reported to be over one hundred years old, but I am afraid that this reflects the difficulty of getting accurate figures more than it does remarkable longevity. One of them is probably ninety; indeed, her family were insistent on the accuracy of the estimate, saying her age had been certified and offered in testimony once in a court of law. The other two great-grandparents were seventy-five and seventy-six. Grandparents are generally fifty or over. Of sixty-one individuals only seven grandparents were in their forties. The parents range in age from nineteen years to sixty-four; the younger families have the younger children, the older families the more mature children. The children range from four months of age to twenty-nine years. There is a surprising number of unmarried youths in their twenties: eleven girls and four boys. It is noteworthy that the unmarried girls are mostly from the richer families and have had extensive schooling.

TABLE 13

DISTRIBUTION OF MEMBERS OF FOUR GENERATIONS
IN EXTENDED VERTICAL FAMILIES

Generation	Number of Individuals
Great-grandparental	4
Grandparental	61
Parental	84
Children	84

In the extended vertical families, how many are essentially nuclear with grandparent(s) or young-married-child-with-spouse increment, or some other degree relative present? [2] If we look for a core in each household, we find that twenty-four households do indeed have a nuclear family center, that is, a pair of spouses and their children. Eleven households do *not* contain a nuclear family core. Those with such a core include these increments: two households with a maternal grandmother; two, a paternal grandmother; two, a paternal grandfather; and one a set of maternal grandparents. Two more have a maternal and a paternal grandfather each, plus a sibling of the grandparent. No preference is indicated for either the maternal or paternal line nor is it necessary that the old person be a direct forebear of the household head or spouse. There are, then, nine households with grandparental generation increments.

Of the ten families with increments of grandchildren, two households have a daughter's son but neither the daughter nor her husband are in the household; in one instance the child stays with his grandparents to attend school; in the other, the boy's mother is in Manila as a maid. I have no information on the child's father; it may be a case of illegitimacy. In a third household, a daughter's two boys are the grandchildren; the daughter and her husband are dead. In only one household is the married child a male, a son in his twenties. His wife and a young child under three also live in the house. Three households contain a married daughter with a child under one year of age. The remaining three households with an increment of grandchildren include an unwed daughter and her child.

While the cases are few, there seems to be a preference for living with the girl's parents while her child is an infant. This probably means that she stays in, or comes back to, her home for childbirth, at least for the birth of her first child. Data on the time in their married life when young married children set up their own residence was obtained by a review of the fifty-nine intact nuclear families. Only three sets of parents had children *under* three. Very few young married couples, then, set up neolocal residence until they have a child or children of their own. There are five households with a nuclear family core and increments other than grandparents or grandchildren; these households shelter a parent's sibling(s) and the child or children of the parent's sibling(s).

Among the extended vertical families, let us examine the parental sibling situation. The eight cases fail to reveal a preferential pattern: wife's brother two, wife's sister three, husband's sister two, and husband's brother one. The extended vertical families range from poor to prosperous and have a wide range of occupations from laborer through teacher.

SKIPPED GENERATION EXTENDED VERTICAL

There were four cases. One was one of the village midwives, a woman reported to be eighty, who lived with her mother's sister's son's son's son and daughter of fourteen and thirteen, respectively. Another was a woman of eighty who lived with her daughter's daughter and son of twenty and twelve, respectively. Another were a couple in their sixties with whom their son's son, aged eight, was living. The last was another couple who referred to the wife's sister's daughter's son, aged fifteen, in their household as an adopted child.

In all the cases, the young people performed a real and necessary function for the oldsters. They helped them with the numerous tasks of procuring water and fuel, carrying loads of produce, and the cleaning and the food preparation which are the daily tasks of life.

TRUNCATED OR RESIDUAL

Truncated or residual families are not so fortunate. Nine households are composed wholly of one or two elderly members with no young people to help them. No member is under forty-four years of age and most are considerably older. These people include the childless and those whose children have died or have left them or have not asked them to join their household. Five households are comprised of a single old lady, each very poor, two selling firewood for a little cash, the other three doing equally poorly recompensed tasks. One receives some help from her children. Three households include husband and wife and the ninth is a brother and sister. In summary, see Table 14.

TABLE 14

FAMILY COMPOSITION OF 129 HOUSEHOLDS

Type of Family	Number in Village
Intact nuclear	59
Truncated nuclear	9
Re-established nuclear	4
Extended horizontal	5
Extended vertical	35
Skipped generation extended vertical	4
Truncated	9
Idiosyncratic	4
Total	129

DISCUSSION

An analysis of household and family composition was necessary for several reasons. First, it was desirable to determine the types of households, the very designation of the term types entailing certain problems. The first to be considered is methodological. The classification of residence systems or the designation of family composition in given households and in given locales has occupied many writers. This attention is a tradition and it is incumbent on any fieldworker to collect data on such matters as residence choice at time of marriage and at other points in the individual developmental cycle. Nonetheless, such collection has not been handled with sufficient systematic care to increase maximally the comparability of the units, or social systems.

The point at which anthropologists have been most lax is in failing to clarify the nature of the operations undertaken in order to describe the unit. The need for greater explication of precisely what takes place in processing data was dramatically revealed when two anthropologists, within a short time of each other, surveyed the same village. Fischer, who, after a three-year lapse classified the village as to residence types, was surprised to find that he had substantial differences in his statements from those made by the first investigator.[3] Although he corrected for changes in the demography of the village in the three-year interval, this procedure failed to bring their conflicting accounts into any closer accord. What had happened? Goodenough, the first investigator, explained that at least two things had happened.

First, the two men had used additional information about the society when interpreting the census data. Census material is not sufficient in itself to allow one to make statements about the nature of the residence types. Accordingly, in the processing of data an investigator brings additional ethnographic information to bear in order to arrive at decisions about certain households. Such a procedure is taken for granted, but that it leaves room for individual interpretation and error has not been emphasized.

Second, Fischer and Goodenough had been working from somewhat different concepts of residence. Goodenough points out the need for concepts which are independent of criteria in any particular culture.[4] This is an important point which has been taken up by many other writers. Goodenough is widely cited both in the United States and among the British anthropologists. There is one point of procedure, however, with which I take issue, concerning the collection of the raw census data. Of this, Goodenough says, "Fischer's and my conclusions were both based on accepted census procedure."[5] It is my contention that we should not presume that we have an "accepted census procedure." Rather, it is incumbent upon us to state only what information we asked for, whom we asked, and the nature of our sample. This I have endeavored to do.

The designation of types of households has another facet. Bohannan has also written on the classification of residences. He states that considerable dissatisfaction with residence classification probably stems from the fact that we have only one such system, that is, the system based on the location of married couples vis-à-vis the kinsmen of one another. He points out that another possible classification stems from a distinction often forgotten by anthropologists — the distinction between families and households.[6]

I do not think that this distinction is often forgotten but rather that it is extremely difficult to make. The difficulty is traceable to a number of complications. The first is that, analytically speaking, an individual belongs to several families. Minimally, the normal married adult is a member of a family of orientation and procreation. In addition, he may be a member of a polygamous family (two or more nuclear families connected by plural marriages, that is, by having one married parent in common) or an extended family (two or more nuclear families connected through an extension of the parent child relationship, that is, by joining the nuclear family of a married adult to that of his or her parents).[7] Furthermore, he may be a member of a clan, and such groupings have also been indiscriminately referred to as families. Therefore, due to this overlapping family membership, a distinction between family and household is apt to be a complex matter.

A second consideration is who is going to be our referent ego in describing a given household. Usually, there is more than one individual in a household. If but one individual were in a household, we could speak of his families without an unduly long and cumbersome description. He might be a widower and belong to a family of procreation as well as orientation, and, possibly, also a polygamous or extended family. But when the household is composed of five members, then plural family membership becomes a different matter for each. This may be obvious when stated, but it is often overlooked. For instance, if the household includes father, mother, and three young male children, the children belong to no family of procreation and may have membership in an extended family either through the mother or father, or through both, depending on the descent rules. In any event, the multiple family membership of the child may differ from the families of his parent(s).

A third factor which arises when considering the distinction between family and household is the criterion or criteria to family membership. Descent and residence are two such common criteria and they may well represent not only different but variant dimensions. That is, the main body of the descent group may or may not reside together. A third criterion, density of interaction of members, may well yield yet a third group, possibly smaller in numbers and probably overlapping among the individuals comprising the members, who may be referred to as a family.

As the foregoing illustrates, the processes of data gathering and data analysis in this important area of family definition have not been thoroughly explored. Perhaps, when designating local groups, most of us tend to take the spatially restricted group — and most commonly the spatial restriction is the shelter walls — and use this as our focal unit of investigation.

An interesting concept, *local* or *domestic groups*, has been developed among the British anthropologists. As early as 1949, Meyer Fortes noted that spread in composition of domestic groups (this would correspond to my household groups) does not mean that the variants are deviants from a model or ideal type but rather that families go through phases of development.[8] In a later writing he developed this idea and spoke of three phases that the normal family would experience.[9] These phases, which may overlap, are expansion, *fission*, and *replacement*. The phase of expansion lasts from marriage until the completion of the family of procreation. It is biologically limited by the wife's fertility. In this phase all the children are economically, affectively, and jurally dependent upon their parents. The phase of fission begins with the marriage of the oldest child and continues until all children are married. The phase of replacement ends with the death of the parents and the replacement in the social structure of the family they founded by families of their children. Here, then, is another and a most insightful way to look into the nature and composition of a family.

Of course, any definition, or, for that matter any classification, is written by a researcher with specific purposes in mind. Various writers have urged greater precision of unit of reference for one purpose or another, especially when that unit is a family or a household group.[10] Levy and Fallers have voiced an interest close to that which motivated my own field work. They argue that the concept of family is of primary interest to social scientists as a structural unit, the main function of which is the socialization of the children. They further argue that

The concept "family," to be useful for general comparative purposes, should be used to refer not to a single social unit in each society, but rather to any small, kinship-structured unit which carries out aspects of the relevant functions. We suspect that, using the term in this way, one would find in most societies a series of "family" units.[11]

As we have already seen, "a series of family units" is precisely what the Leyte village contained. However, the series of units that Levy and Fallers were referring to was not the varieties of household types but rather structural functional units in the sense that one might distinguish between an economic unit and a socialization unit.

I find this difficulty with their strictures. They ask that a fieldworker designate the various units which are responsible for socializing each child for designated portions of its life. It may or may not be possible to do this. In Guinhangdan, it is not the parents, nor yet the parents and siblings, not yet the parents, siblings, and secondary kin, but all of these *and* tertiary kin *and* neighbors *and* any villager who comes into contact with the child who contributes to his socialization. Another weakness of their argument is that while they are fighting for a better definition of family, they are assuming that we all know what "socialization" is. They fail to specify whether by socialization they mean a general orientation, a series of specific behaviors in specific situations (teaching, punishing, spending time with the child, loving the child), or whatever they may have had in mind.

In summary, I suggest that little has been done to explore the complexity of household composition and offer my findings in a Philippine village as evidence that it may be far more complex than has been assumed in our classifications heretofore. I would also suggest that we ought to examine the reasons for our investigation of residences and see whether we have different bases for investigation now than have been traditional. At least some of us are more interested in the environment of the child than we are in the kinship structure per se. With this orientation, it is more important to know more about the household group, its make-up and influence, than it is to investigate at length preferential marriage patterns, residence at or after marriage, and naming and inheritance procedures.

5: Mother and Child in Guinhangdan

FAMILY and kin impinge on the individual earlier and more continuously than does any other agency of socialization. From the moment of birth and throughout the lifetime of an individual, the influence of siblings and secondary and tertiary kin are almost incalculable in total effect. The parents and siblings, as well as the spouse and children of any particular person, comprise the *primary* relatives. In Murdock's terms, the Mo and Fa and Si's and Br's in the family of orientation and the Wi or Hu and the So's and Da's in the family of procreation are the primary relatives of a given Ego.[1] Each primary relative is, in turn, an Ego with primary relatives of his own. The primary relatives of the second Ego are, for the most part, the *secondary* relatives of the first. Theoretically, a person may have thirty-three kinds of secondary relatives. As we will not deal with them exhaustively, several examples will clarify: FaFa, FaMo, FaSi, FaBr, MoFa, MoMo, MoSi, MoBr, BrWi, BrSo, BrDa, SiHu, SiSo, SiDa, and the spouses of children and children's children. For tertiary relatives there are 151 possibilities and these include eight great-grandparents, eight first cousins, and the spouses of all aunts, uncles, nieces, and nephews.

In Guinhangdan, descent is bilateral in the sense that a growing child learns to think of himself as related equally to the kin of his mother and father. It is not possible for either practical or analytical purposes to mark the kin boundaries vertically or horizontally. Actually, the kin who are meaningful and effective differ from individual to individual and from period to period within the lifetime of any given individual.[2] Kin relationships are not only a biological but also a social phenomenon. Unless the biological fact of relationship is reinforced by acts of responsibility and privilege between the individuals involved, the relationship is not a significant one for them. Kin with whom one does not communicate and who are not accessible cease to function in the web of reciprocal privileges and responsibilities which are basic to the system. Lynch and Evangelista found, and I can corroborate, that the names of kin from some distant village may not be known.[3] Unless the accident of consanguinity or affinity is validated by social interaction, the kinship tie is not an effective bond.

In Guinhangdan, marriage is monogamous as it is throughout most of the Philippines. Residence at the time of marriage is a complex matter. Normally, the young couple joins an established household for the first few years of married life, but the factors which decide whose household that shall be are not the degree of closeness of the relationship nor yet whether the connection is in the male or female line. What seems to be operative here are two factors: the need of one of the sets of parents (and/or other degree relative) for the labor and/or financial aid of the young couple; and, second, a strong personal need on the part of a parent or set of parents (or other degree relative) for the presence of his or her child. In the latter instance, the possessive parent must have the manipulative power to persuade or coerce the couple to take up residence with him or her. Later, when the young married people can afford a residence of their own, they build a house; normally, by this time they have a child or two. In the course of the development of the family, more children will probably be born and then, late in the cycle, an aged and/or widowed parent will often join the household of a married child.[4] Thus the system of residence has a pattern which Lynch has called neolocal with provision for utrolocal at the beginning of married life and again in later years.[5]

We shall first discuss the system of kinship terminology with reference both to the vocative and referential systems; then mention the artificial kin systems, both those created by marriage and by other ceremonial alliances; and, finally, considerable attention will be given to the behavior patterns appropriate between different kin.

TERMINOLOGY

Beginning with the family of orientation and ego's relationship to the second ascending generation, we shall work downward in generation, through the family of procreation to the second descending generation, then move outward to affinal relatives and artificially created kin.

Kroeber has shown that one of the determinants of kinship terminology is whether the relation is through the male or the female line.[6] This principle does not operate in Guinhangdan and the terminology shows no distinctions. Nor is there any distinction, terminologically, as to the sex of the speaker. The term used by either a male or a female for MoMo, FaMo, MoFa, and FaFa is *apoy*, a term both vocative and referential. Apoy is also applicable to siblings of grandparents.

In the first ascending generation, the terms used for secondary relations are more varied. The choice of a term for MoBr, MoSi, FaBr, and FaSi differs slightly from situation to situation, the most important criterion being age and next, the degree of affection between the pair. If the person addressed or referred to is very much older than the speaker he may be called apoy. If he is near the father's age he will be addressed and called *bata*, a female *dada*. I suspect, but am not certain, that these are the most frequently used terms. If he is nearer in age to elder siblings of Ego, he will be called *mano*, or, if female, *mana*. Parent's siblings may be addressed or referred to by parental terms. A wide variety of personal names with affectionate endings and nicknames are also used. Father is generally addressed as *tatay*; mother as *nanay*. Alternate terms are *tata* and *tatang*, and *nana* and *nanang*. The reference terms are *amay*, father, and *iroy*, mother. Some use is made of terms from English, *mamah* and *papah* for address and reference.

A spouse is referred to as *asawa* and generally called by name, diminutive, or nickname. Older brother is addressed and referred to as mano; older sister is mana. Younger siblings of either sex are referred to as *bugtu*. *Manghud* is a reference term for any younger person, relative or not. Female younger siblings are addressed and occasionally referred to as *iday* but so too are nonrelated younger females. The same is true for *idoiy* and *budoiy* for males. The last three have a more generic meaning of the little one and are generally uttered in an affectionate tone.

Tertiary relatives such as FaBrSo, FaSiSo, FaBrDa, FaSiDa, MoSiDa, MoBrDa, MoBrSo, and MoSiSo are referred to collectively and individually as *patud*. In addressing them age becomes a factor and they may be called mano or mana or patud.

In the first descending generation, male issue of any age and regardless of birth order are addressed by name, nickname, diminutive, or budoiy and idoiy; the same is true for female issue except that the generic affectionate term of address is iday. *Anak* means "child of ———— " and is a general reference term without reference to sex, relation to ego, age, or relation of ego to parent. *Omangkon* is the reference term for niece, nephew, or child of a cousin of any degree. The term of address is the first name or nickname. Addressing children with diminutives is dropped when they are adult children.

In the second descending generation, one's own grandchildren and those of siblings and cousins are called by name, nickname, budoiy, or iday. *Apo* or *apo nga* plus name are the terms of reference.

Various ceremonial alliances increase one's family members; the most common and most important of these being marriage. Spouses in the grandparental generation are apoy; both reference and address. All remaining in-law terms to be discussed are in the referential system. Names and nicknames are used in address. Parent's sibling's husbands are bata and tatay. Parent's sibling's wives are dada and nanay. A wife calls her parents-in-law by the same term as does her husband. Since there are two (or perhaps three different sets of terms), her address and reference will vary. The same is true for a man and his parents-in-law. SiHu is *bayaw*; BrWi is *hipag*. SoWi or DaHu are *umaged* or *umaged nga* plus name. The male spouses of cousins are bayaw, or a variant such as *bayaw haig patud*, the female, hipag. The spouses of grandchildren, sibling's grandchildren, and cousin's grandchildren are umaged nga apo, or apo where specificity is not needed.

While marriage is a ceremonial alliance that affects kin membership for as many generations as are extant, or as can be remembered, there is another system in which artificial kin relationships are created which affect only one or two generations. This is the sponsor or godparent system brought into play at baptism, confirmation, and marriage. A sponsored child is related to the sponsor, the sponsor's spouse, and their children, but that is all; the same is true of a sponsored bride. The parents of a sponsored child are related to the sponsors but neither to the sponsor's parents or children. Cosponsors who were not related prior to the ceremony become related to their cosponsor and his spouse, but that is all.

Whether a sponsor becomes a sponsor at baptism, confirmation, or marriage, the terminology is the same. The terms of address applicable to a sponsor and his or her spouse are the mother-father (nanay-tatay) terms. The terms of address are nanay plus name and tatay plus name; the terms of reference are *kompadreh* and *komadreh*. Children of a sponsor are addressed and referred to as *ogtu*. Two sets of parents who become related through the sponsorship of one of their children call each other *madi* and *padi* and refer to each other as kompadreh and komadreh.

An excellent study of age and sex roles in a Philippine village has been made by Agaton P. Pal.[7] The village studied by Dr. Pal was Esperanza in the municipality of Matalom on the southwestern coast of Leyte. Leyte is an island province and the people as a whole share many aspects of social organization and culture. At the same time, the presence of a mountain barrier which is the backbone of the island accounts, in part, for regional differences within the island. Thus, the dialect spoken in western Leyte is called *Walay*. The mutual intelligibility between speakers of Walay on the west coast and Waray Waray on the east coast is 50 per cent.[8]

Dr. Pal finds that there are five age categories which are distinguished from one another in barrio Esperanza. These are not, of course, distinguished from one another solely on the basis of age, but on the basis of characteristics closely associated with age.[9] He finds that there is a term for infant which is applicable up to about the age of five. There is another for a child of from approximately five to fifteen years, a third for the adolescent of from roughly fifteen to twenty-five years of age; and one for the adult of from twenty-five to fifty-five years of age and a fifth for the old folks of fifty-five and over.[10]

My own data based on an informal session with three informants and on the terms used to address or refer to certain individuals in daily intercourse leads me to agree with the basic subdivision of the village population. In addition, and here there is some divergence from Pal's usage, in Guinhangdan the term *pulahay* or *puya* is used to refer to a newly born baby. Bata is generic for child and may be used from infancy to adolescence. A *daragita* is a female of about nine to eighteen years of age and a *daraga* is an unmarried female older than eighteen but not yet a spinster. An *olitawohay* is a male of about nine to eighteen years of age and an *olitaw* is a male over eighteen and unmarried. *Inasawan* may be used to refer to either of a pair of spouses and *lagas* is an aged male or female.

As Pal points out, the only age period during which the sex of

the actor is terminologically differentiated is in the period of adolescence, at which time not only are the sexes differentiated but also
the time of adolescence is divided into late and early.[11] This reflects
the disinterest of the society in sex as a feature of role except in the
adolescent period. Or, perhaps it would be more accurate to say the
lack of emphasis on sex as a determinant of role is reflected in the
terminology of all periods except the adolescent.

The terms given in the present report are the most simple and the
most general. Many variations exist but I did not attempt the kind of
study necessary to establish a norm and variation on kinship terms
and usages. For instance, Homans and Schneider [12] point out that a
fundamental characteristic of the American system is the presence of
a wide variety of alternate terms for kinsmen. They found that in
the referential system a term might be modified by a possessive pro-
noun, or in reference to person spoken to, or with situational context. The variations revolve around two axes: an ordering or classifying aspect and a role or relationship-designating aspect. Such
axes of variation exist in Guinhangdan, but whereas in America
personal aspects of the role relationship are of primary importance,[13]
in the village the classifying or ordering aspect is emphasized. The
individual characteristics of role players are subordinated to class
membership, and perception of membership in a particular class
is strongly influenced by the age of the member in relation to ego.

MOTHER-TO-CHILD RELATIONSHIPS: SOURCE MATERIAL

A carefully structured interview schedule was adopted from Whiting's *Field Guide for a Study of Socialization in Five Societies*. With
minor alterations the interview was administered to nineteen wom-
en, seven of whom were pretests. The remaining twelve women were
deliberately chosen to represent as much variability in socioeconomic status as is possible with such a limited sample. The structured interview schedule had been written in English. In the village I had it
translated to the native language, Waray Waray, by one worker and
then retranslated to English by another. The original version and
the derived translation were then compared; discrepancies were
noted, questioned, adjusted, and greater fidelity to original intent
and meaning were achieved. The adopted schedule can be found in
the Appendix.

In the seven pretests, as well as in later interviews, every effort
was made to keep the interview situation uniform. For instance, the

mother, the interpreter, and the anthropologist met in the house or on the porch of the respondent's home. No interviews were given outdoors or while the mother was occupied in any activity other than answering the question. It was suggested tentatively that other family members leave, but if they wished to stay, nothing further was said. With the high premium placed on sociability and gregariousness in the Philippines, it was not tactful to insist on the ideal interview situation of mother, interpreter, and investigator. The native tongue was used in all interviews, including those in which the mother spoke English fluently. Questions were presented in strict order with standardized probes with as little extraneous explanation as possible.

Information was gathered about six male and six female children ranging in age from three to ten. The economic level of the families ranged from poor to prosperous and included laborers, copra growers, tenant farmers, fishermen, and a teacher. Ten of the children were living in a nuclear family household, but in one household the father had been dead for four years and in another the father's mother also lived in the house. The number of children in the household ranged from one to seven. The variation achieved in family composition included one family with an only child, three families with three children, two families with four children, two families with five children, three families with six children, and one family with seven children. Only living children were counted. Three of the families had all girls; two had only boys. Four of the children about whom the mothers were questioned were the oldest in their families, three were the youngest, and five were middle children. Although the mothers were chosen to represent variability in socioeconomic status and family composition, the present report is not oriented to individual differences. The information which is presented is the result of an attempt to portray the customary behaviors and some alternate permissible actions. Differences in custom according to the age or sex of the child are mentioned. Some comparison is made with American children.

The following system of processing was used: All responses relevant to a particular variable were abstracted and studied. Topical, descriptive material bearing on the behavior studied was also consulted. Finally, descriptive and summary statements were written.

MOTHER-TO-CHILD RELATIONSHIPS:
FINDINGS — SUCCORANCE TRAINING

Child-training practices may be studied in many ways. The data in this study are oriented to seven systems of behavior, first formulated by Whiting *et al.*[14]

Personality is a complicated phenomenon which also may be studied in many ways. To give the reader some idea of Whiting's and his associates' thought on personality, I include the chart on relationships below. (See Fig. 8.)

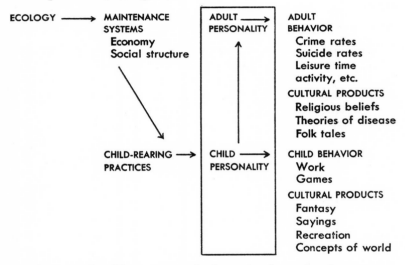

Fig. 8. A simplified conceptual scheme for the study of patterns of child rearing and manifestations of personality characteristics.

Whiting points out that personality may only be inferred. One fruitful and useful way to look at both the manifestations of personality and the relationship between childhood experiences and adult characteristics is presented very simply in this figure. In this formulation, the researchers conceptualize that ecology, economy, technology, and other manifestations of social structure set the parameters of behavior of the agents of child rearing. The child-rearing practices in turn increase the number of children with a certain kind of "child personality." The child's personality is much (or little?) related to the "adult personality." Both "personalities" are expressed in and may be observed in other manifestations of culture. On the adult level, these include crime and suicide rates, leisure-time activities, religious beliefs, theories of disease, and oral literature. On the child level, one might study work patterns, games, and the mental life as inferred from fantasy, and concepts of the child's world. In *Six Cultures: Studies of Child Rearing*, Whiting states that the causal relationships cannot be known from our present knowledge and that discussion of such relationships will end with a problem similar to that on the chicken or the egg.

Let us begin with a simpler problem: the observation of behavior system.

SUCCORANCE

Succorance is defined as tendencies to await or to signal for and accept the nurturant response of another. Succorance is a state of dependency characteristic of infancy but is also present in the growing and grown organism. When the organism is in tension, a number of behaviors may be produced.

In Guinhangdan the mother is the primary, but by no means the only, caretaker of the infant and the young child. Occasionally, a family is so poor that the mother must work in the fields, and the grandparent of either sex or a grandparental or parental sibling may be the main caretaker. However, responsibility for the child is not the primary concern of a single individual. The father helps a good deal in feeding, bathing, and general surveillance. A child's elder siblings, nearby kin, and neighbors assume a continuing active part in caring for the child, not as a distinct activity but as an undifferentiated, integral part of daily life.

Succorance in the infant may be expressed in face or posture, cry or whimper. The older child may use these forms of communication plus phrases and sentences to signal for the nurturant response of another. In the village, tendencies to succorance are highly and fairly consistently rewarded for the first five years of life. When an infant cries, regardless of what the reason may be, the mother's response tendency is to nurse him. She may take additional steps to comfort him, such as changing rags or bedding if they are wet or soiled, or the child is sung to, cuddled, or rocked in the bamboo hammock. The mother is not the only one to respond to the child's cries. To the very young baby, anyone in the room will act nurturantly. A sibling as young as five may hold, rock, or murmur to the child.

Continued crying of the unweaned child is not unfailingly rewarded by attention, however. Should the infant nurse until satiated and then cry again, he is allowed to cry because it is believed that it is "good for a fed child to cry." Another consideration relevant to the strength of a succorance system of behavior is the promptness with which signals of need are answered. When questioned about the quickness with which they would respond to a crying baby, mothers unanimously answered "immediately" or "quickly." However, observation establishes that this is not literally true. When women are busy with food preparation or some specialized task which they may not easily leave, they let the child cry, or ask a sibling to tend him.

Succorant tendencies in an older child may often be noted in a bid for attention or aid. For example, the child may ask the mother to make a cloth doll or a kite, reach for something, or help close a button. Usually the mother will help the child, but if she thinks he can perform the requested action himself, she will not, in most instances, aid him; she will not nurture for nurturance's sake. Succorant behavior may be exhibited when the child slips, stumbles, or falls. The mother picks him up and murmurs consolingly. When the fall results in a possible sprain or break, the child is brought to the *hilot* or curer for examination and treatment.

To summarize: most mothers respond nurturantly to a crying child; the quickness with which they respond varies with the pressure of work which must be done and, to a lesser degree, with the intensity of their individual nurturant tendencies. Work has priority for rich and poor alike. The children of poorer parents (who put more time and energy into sheer survival activities) will be less quickly and less frequently nurtured by the mother and other socializing agents than will the child in a family which is more prosperous or which has many workers. The age of the child is an important factor and the child past the infant years is less permissively treated when the parents are busy with the rudiments of subsistence than is the younger child. At best, the older child will be forced to wait until the household task or field work is completed.

ACHIEVEMENT AND RESPONSIBILITY TRAINING

Achievement consists of ability to see one's self as an actor, tendencies to evaluate one's behavior and that of others in reference to standards of excellence and endeavors to behave so as to merit a high rank on the scale of excellence. In any situation in which performance of an act, utterance of a phrase, or assumption of an attitude are clearly expected of ego, *responsibility* is the realization of the expectation. Responsibility consists of tendencies to be ready, willing and able to fulfill one's obligations, both implicit and explicit. Achievement and responsibility are related variables. Both encompass abilities which are more characteristic of the growing or grown organism but which also may be present in the normal young child in the course of his development and maturation.

Data about training for achievement and the assumption of responsibility are organized around feeding, dressing, and playing away from home. The concept of deliberate training undertaken at a certain age with a goal of achievement at a somewhat later age is missing in the village. Children are regarded as helpless and lovable innocents who gradually grow up and, somehow, in the same slow process, begin to exhibit certain natural maturative abilities. The cultural ideal prescribes that performance of these abilities should not be hurried.

Thus, not only are children not urged to stand or to walk; they are also discouraged and restrained from early or, what is presumed, premature, efforts to do so.

Obtaining the specific age at which a child begins to walk, talk, or feed himself is difficult because Filipino mothers are not time minded. They are not geared to an ordering of events by the clock and calendar but are attuned to subtle variations of day and season. Neither are they accustomed to note actions in sequences and to mentally record changes. Therefore, when the mother is pressed to say at what age her child could feed himself, the answer, generally, is "two years," or "three years." The timing of the accomplishment is not important.[15]

The age at which children are able to dress themselves ranges from two to six, although most are considered able by two or three. The late age at which some children become independent in dressing is surprising, particularly when it is noted that the only item of clothing which the children wear is a shirt or dress pulled over the head.

Another measure of achievement and responsibility training is the degree to which the child is freed from the mother's presence. Once the child has achieved enough mobility to leave the mother or caretaker, he begins to extend his area of exploration into the yard and grounds surrounding the house. He may be allowed to leave the house for an hour or two each day in the company of a sibling. The child from the ages of two to four begins to roam further and to go into paths, streets, and neighboring grounds.

Early efforts at accomplishment are not usually rewarded with verbal recognition. Before long, the performance of some recent achievement is taken for granted and only its nonperformance elicits parental reaction. What conscious teaching of the young there is occurs primarily by example, and the children learn by imitating. When verbal instructions accompany the example, the socializing agent speaks quietly. The ideal speech pattern for a socializing agent is a modulated tone, a low-pitched voice, and a gentle, coaxing manner.[16] Quietly, a mother coaxes a child to some performance, often using *budoiy* (dear little boy) or *iday* (nice little girl) as incentive. Sometimes an elder sibling is held up as an example.

For further information on achievement and responsibility, mothers were asked about the child's part in ordinary household tasks. Children under five can help carry water; gather, carry, and stack fuel; sweep a floor with a short, wide, fanlike broom; and polish the floor by cupping a bare foot over half a coconut husk and skating around on it. By the time a child is six or seven, baby care is added to his participation in the growing up roles. Carrying messages to relatives and neighbors and securing salt or soap from the neighborhood store are soon part of the children's activities. Finally, washing the dishes, sweeping the dirt yards, caring for chickens, pigs, and goats are learned before they are ten. Palm-leaf sewing and helping with the harvest start about eight or ten. No distinctions are made as to sex for any of these performances.[17]

The level of competence which mothers expect of their children in the performance of a task is of interest. By and large, achievement level is unimportant. Mothers are content if the work is done and are not concerned about how it is done. There are practical and valid reasons why they do not think about competence as a characteristic: the tasks are simple and do not require a great deal of ability or perserverance to carry out; a child is not asked to perform a task beyond his ability; and a performance is only superficially evaluated; that is, it is performed or not performed. However, if in the course of the execution of a chore the child wastes something or hurts someone, notice is taken. The child who is careless and spills rice or who hurts himself in stacking wood will be judged, not in reference to a level of competence, but by the results of his act. He is more apt to be scolded for the consequences of his inept action than for the ineptness itself. Mothers are sometimes calm about carelessness and either overlook the incident or explain patiently; but some mothers scold, reprimand, or pinch the errant child.

In summary, it may be said that standards of excellence of performance are not established or maintained. When it is noticeable that the work is ineptly performed, it frequently passes unnoticed or without comment, but sometimes the child may be shown again what is expected of him. If the child is stubborn or resistant to repeated attempts to teach him, scolding and corporal punishment follow. Neither self-reliance, responsibility, nor achievement are emphasized as systems of behavior.

OBEDIENCE TRAINING

Obedience consists of tendencies to conform to hints, suggestions, requests, or demands that some course of action be carried out or some attitude be displayed. In situations in which obedience is involved, the other actor is acting dominantly.

When a village child has been asked to do something and he pretends not to hear or to understand occasionally, the mother lets the matter drop. If the child dawdles or delays he will most likely be chided. If he continues to procrastinate, and the mother to insist, her impatience increases and she may change her tactics from coaxing or threatening to pinching or slapping. The children do what they are told to do most of the time if the socializer is insistent enough. However, they do procrastinate a good deal.

The question may be raised as to whether the mother is consistent in the action she takes when the child fails to obey. Very few, if any, village mothers are invariably consistent. Depending on a complex set of variables including the mother's mood, the child's mood, and the recent interaction patterns of both, the child may be permitted to escape, allowed to sulk, or be punished. This inconsistency is a contributing factor to the evasiveness of the children. Other factors are the many demands put upon them and the excessive number of people to whom they are subject in the authority structure.

In summary, obedience and respect from anyone younger to anyone older is a highly valued behavior system. Disobedience and disrespect are punished most of the time once the child has reached the age of five which is considered to be an "age of reason," a time when the child can discriminate among significant others and be held more responsible for his acts. For the first five years the child is greatly indulged, but even in this period a high premium is placed on submissive, deferent, and respectful behavior to older siblings, parents, and others.

SOCIABILITY TRAINING

Sociability consists of tendencies to make friendly responses and to engage in activities with others merely for the sake of gregariousness. While sociability may be present in interaction between ego and superordinate or ego and subordinate, it is most clearly discerned in action among peers. Between superordinate and ego, the action is likely to take on aspects of succorance, and between ego and subordinate, aspects of nurturance, particularly if the other actor is needy or resourceful.

Training for sociability must be in reference to the group with which one is being trained to be sociable. In Guinhangdan, this includes the nuclear and extended family but beyond that, group boundaries shift and flow. On the whole, village mothers want their children to play alone, with siblings, or kin. The circumscription of play groups is rationalized in a number of ways. First, the youngsters may become embroiled in a quarrel; second, if the child is playing away from home, he is inaccessible for the many small work demands put upon him in the course of the day; third, the mother may not approve of the personalities and habits of the other children and remove her child from the influence of such possible role models.

To have the child play alone or with a few family intimates is the expressed ideal. In actuality, the children seek out other children without regard for kin ties. They play with neighbors' children, with children of families whom their families may wish to avoid or whom they may consider "enemies." Very young children everywhere are remarkably uncommitted to the prejudices, passions, and convictions of their elders. As they grow older, children begin to observe some restriction on their choice of playmates in accord with parental wishes.

Play groups tend to be structured by age. Toddlers and early walkers play together regardless of sex. At about the age of five, the children begin to segregate into all male or female groups. Children seldom play alone; they are almost always in groups. Games are both formal and spontaneous.

In summary, sociability is a highly valued behavior system. Mothers are ambivalent concerning with whom their child shall be sociable when the other actor is not a family member. Sociability with one's own family members is always desirable; sociability to nonfamily members may be desirable, depending on the immediate circumstances of the two families in relation to each other.

DOMINANCE AND AGGRESSION TRAINING

Dominance consists of tendencies to direct the acts of others and to enforce compliance and obedience in others. Dominance may be subtle or overt. One may attempt to direct another without making open or formal demands, or consciously and autocratically seek to enforce one's will on others. *Aggression* consists of tendencies to act with intent to hurt another. Aggression may be expressed in attitude, posture, speech, or action. Physical aggression is often only a small part of the whole. Aggression may be expressed verbally by teasing, ridiculing, reprimanding, scolding, jeering, threatening, cursing, or otherwise abusing vocally.

In Guinhangdan, the mother will punish rather than encourage any incipient self-assertiveness in her young one. If her children's requests for aid become demands, she hardens against them.

Children's attempts at dominance in the play group are met with mixed reactions. Mothers take some pride in the child's assertiveness but such pride is overshadowed by cultural ideals that a child be quiet, meek, submissive, and obedient. Such behavior must be encouraged and the reverse discouraged regardless of personal feelings.[18] It is another ideal that peace and harmony be maintained among all village families, and when tranquility is rent by quarrels among children, their dominant or aggressive behavior is legitimate cause for punishment. The emphasis on obedience, submission, and nonaggression is related to a lack of training for leadership. Leadership is defined as "bossiness." "Bossy" children are admonished to be mild and kind, and told not to seek to impose their will on smaller children and playmates. (Among adults, the work members of a certain kind of fishing venture are formed when the "followers" seek out the "leader.")

If conflict breaks out in the play group, the mother may take at least two courses. She may remove her offspring from the fray and urge the others to go home; or she may inquire into the cause of the quarrel and, as a result of her investigation, punish one or more of the children, some of them not her own. If a child is trying to dominate the other children, he will probably be punished. This applies to males and females and to all of the age groups studied. Furthermore, mothers are unanimous in agreeing that children who have been the target for aggression should not fight back. Accordingly, children are not encouraged in bellicose behavior and, in fact, are punished for it. "I even whip him whenever I learn that he has been in a quarrel."

Aggression in the play group is deplored and suppressed; against elders it is intolerable. Classed with disobedience, it is often part of a sequence of events initiated in a noncompliant action. Such sequences have several patterns. In some instances, the socializer nags the disobedient child until he is subdued into a semblance of submission.[19] Or the socializer may use a number of methods: command, inattention, repetition of command, attempt at escape, capture and punishment; or softly worded requests, bland and obvious inattention, request repeated, attempts at distraction, slow rise of anger, and so on. When a child's disobedience is linked with anger manifestations against its parents, punishments are particularly severe. Striking or kicking an elder sibling or an adult calls for the strongest punishments. The age of the child is not a saving circumstance. Children as young as four have been beaten with a leather belt because of defiance. Punishment for overt aggression to elders is swift. Said one mother, "I don't take time to look for a stick." In summary, aggression and dominance are behavior systems which are not emphasized and manifestations of which are punished.

FORMS OF PUNISHMENT

Teasing is a mild form of verbal aggression which, however, may be delivered in a stinging and irritating manner. The Philippine village child must learn to submit to this social discipline with good grace and, indeed, to develop skill in it. It is interesting to note that among adults, only two roles are permitted in which the teased one may respond aggressively: the witch and the drunk. A common form of verbal coercion is the threat of the *asuang*, a witchlike bogeyman, used early and frequently in a child's life, and effectively for several years. Someone may knock surreptitiously on the walls of the house and say, "Listen, it is the asuang. Do what you are told or he will

get you!" Or, at dusk when asuangs are presumed to prowl, the socializer will use the threat of the witch to bring her wanderers to the
safety of the home.

The denial of a tidbit or a trifle is used as a punishment but it is
not common, nor is the rejection of the child by sending him away
from the presence of the punisher. Rejection by not speaking is rare.
Pinching is widely and frequently used. Kneeling, a practice introduced by the Spanish, is often used as a punishment. Kneeling on
bamboo floors is painful enough but an outraged parent may increase the punishment by putting a few dried peas under the child's
knees or forcing him to stretch out his arms. To spank, according to
Webster, is "to strike, or to strike the buttocks of, with an open
hand." Some, but not all, of this meaning applies to "spanking" as
the word is used, and as the act is practiced in the village. Spanking
is mainly striking the child on the lower legs, thighs, or hands with
the open hand. It is not customary to hit the child on the buttocks.
It is worthwhile noting that there is nothing ritual about any spanking; they are administered quickly and in anger, not planned for or
awaited. Most punishments are spontaneous in the privacy of the
home. To summarize, the main corporal punishments are pinching,
slapping, or striking with the broom. The main verbal punishments
are teasing, joking, and the threat of the witch.

DISCIPLINARIANS

The question of who administers the punishment in the training of the young is related to the more general question of the authority structure within the family. The fact that there is no single
disciplinarian is consonant with other child-rearing practices. Although mother and father are considered as equal in authority, the
mother tends to do more of the actual punishing. In a few cases,
the mother considers herself the chief and sole disciplinarian. In a
lesser number of cases, the father is formally vested with the rights
of punishment, but, conversely, in some families he does not punish at all. It appears that the father's role as disciplinarian is not
routinized but differs from father to father. In some families, he
talks to the errant child, chiding, advising, or scolding but avoiding
corporal punishment. In other families he may spank or beat the
child.

The situation with regard to authority among siblings has been
insightfully described by Stoodley for Tagalog (northern Philip-

pines) families. He notes that authority is structured according to the birth order of the siblings regardless of sex. All older brothers and sisters have authority over all younger ones although in some instances the age difference may be no more than a year. Among the Tagalog families, the oldest sister or brother had special authority. Among the Guinhangdan villagers this was also true, but greater emphasis fell on the oldest sister, who held a position remarkably close to that of the mother in regard to responsibilities and privileges toward her siblings. She was regarded with special respect, not infrequently with fear, and, needless to say, functioned as a disciplinarian. Stoodley uses the felicitous phrase "ladder of authority" to describe the sibling relationships.

. . . each rung of the ladder (represents) a chronological period of one year. A sibling is subject to the authority of any sibling above him on the ladder, but the more rungs that separate him from the other sibling, the more extensive the authority.[20]

The kind of punishment an elder sibling may administer varies with the age gap between the siblings. If a child is sufficiently older than a sibling, he may use corporal punishment, but if he is near the child in age, he will only scold. Severe beatings certainly occur but I have no frequency measures. Stoodley points out that the younger child has the right of appeal; he or she may complain to the parent about punishment which is too harsh or which is not warranted by the age differential of the two.

FORMS OF REWARDS

Rewards among village mothers take many forms. Babies are caressed, fondled, and kissed a good deal, but children of five or six are considered too old for such loving handling. Most mothers praise a child when he has done something particularly pleasing, but many behaviors, particularly in the realm of small achievements, are not noticed at all. Also, some mothers consciously withhold praise, bestowing it only when the child is not present. Others do not praise their offspring at all on the assumption that children (over five) in general are naughty and presumptuous and rare exhibitions of good behavior ought to be overlooked. The favored child may be allowed some privilege which is ordinarily not permitted such as playing beyond a prescribed area, an excursion to the beach, a stroll, a visit, or, rarely, a movie in the city. A frequent reward is the mere promise of some pleasure or treat in the future. A cloth doll, bread, candy, a few *centavos*, or new clothes are important rewards whether as promises or as actualities.

DISCUSSION

The findings will be discussed in relation to the following questions: Is a given behavior system emphasized or de-emphasized? Is the expected and/or customary behavior different for males and females? What, if any, differences are due to the age of the child? In addition, occasional comparison will be made with middle-class American standards.

Succorant tendencies are characteristic of the infant and young child anywhere. However, such tendencies may be ignored, rewarded with attention, or punished. In Guinhangdan succorance is emphasized for both males and females. Until about the age of five, such tendencies are fairly consistently rewarded; after the age of five the child is expected to be less needy. Correlatively, little doubt exists that succorance as a means of interaction is very important to adults. In many situations, propitiation, or merely standing mutely in need, are the proper behavior patterns.

Achievement and responsibility are not emphasized in Guinhangdan, neither for males nor for females, nor for the younger or older child. In fact, the lack of standards of excellence in all child-training practices is notable. Mothers do not compete with each other in the manner so vital and satisfying to the American middle-class mother. We need only recall the lack of interest of the Filipino mother in the age at which her child began to walk, talk, or feed himself.

This may be contrasted with the competitiveness and aggressiveness of American mothers, most of whom know, by the month, if not the week, when their child first lifted up his head, rolled over completely, grasped something and lifted himself up, etc. American mothers urge their babies to stand or walk; the Filipino mother discourages early attempts; the American mother fosters independence; the Filipino mother, dependence. In other words, American mothers are achievement oriented and competitive; Filipino village mothers are not. Neither responsibility, self-reliance, nor achievement can be said to be emphasized and encouraged by the village mother. Village children of both sexes perform many household tasks at a young age, but the impetus to such action is from others — parents, siblings, or kin rather than from themselves. The village children make a necessary contribution to the work routine of the house and field. In contrast, American children, particularly in the age range of three to ten, are not the economic asset to the family as are Filipino children.[21] The majority of American children do not take part in subsistence activities and, consequently, lack both a role in household economy and satisfaction in it. Nonetheless, they are highly achievement oriented.

Previous investigators into the relationship between achievement, measured as a component in the folktales of a people, and the degree of training for independence in the children found that cultures which are concerned with achievement are likely to stress independence training in childhood. They found that all measures of the emphasis on independence in the child are significantly related to the amplitude of the achievement score in the culture. That is, the less the initial indulgence, the earlier the age at which the child is expected to be self-responsible, and the greater the severity of punishment for manifestations of dependence, the greater the achievement score tends to be. The present study tends to confirm this hypothesis.[22]

In a study concerned with differences in child-rearing attitudes of "urban social classes" in the Philippines and with differences between middle-class Philippine and American children, Guthrie used the Schaefer and Bell Parental Attitude Research Instrument. His findings are interesting for comparison. He states that lower-class Philippine mothers are very authoritarian with their children. They strongly stress obedience and suppression of aggression. So thorough is their control that they wish even to know what their children are thinking. In contrast, mothers from higher social groups (also in the Philippines) stress more independence for the child and greater freedom for the mother. The lower-class Philippine mother (and I would suggest the rural Philippine mother, regardless of social class) emphasizes a detailed control of her child, whereas those from the higher classes give the child greater opportunity for self-expression. The study suggests that American mothers approach their role with less confidence and more irritation and frustration at the demands of motherhood. The Philippine mother is more at ease, more pervasively influential and controlling and, also, more supportive of the child in her attitudes.[23]

In Guinhangdan, obedience is a virtue of prime importance. Children of both sexes and all ages are consistently highly obedient to their elders. Such obedience becomes a lifetime habit and may entail many personal sacrifices. In comparison, American children are much less obedient than are the village children.

The information gathered about sociability is not clear. Perhaps this is because behavior with subordinates or superordinates is so much more important to the villager than is behavior with equals. Patterns of deference and respect to elders are emphasized to a much greater degree than patterns with peers. In fact, it is moot whether it can be said that there are patterns which define and give value to equality.

Another feature about sociability in the village is that prescriptions for childhood and for adult years are in conflict. While there is agreement that being a good neighbor is important, children are urged not to play with neighbors but only with kin. In contrast, in adult life neighbors are frequently consulted, sought after, and helped, although they are never viewed with the same trust, nor held in the same regard, as kin. The number of people with which one is supposed to be sociable increases with the age and experience of the individual.

Failure to encourage gregariousness in village children may be contrasted with the training of the American child. In the American middle class, strong emphasis is placed on the integration of the child into his play group (which generally includes no kin); group cooperation and individual adjustment into group goals and activities are primary. Practically no interest in this facet of behavior occurs among village mothers.

Dominant and aggressive behavior is discouraged and suppressed in the village and training for suppression begins very early for both sexes. Quarrels among children are deplored; physical violence is inveighed against; and any attempt at self-assertiveness is discouraged or punished. Mothers are unanimous in deploring the quarrelsome child in the play group and in praising the peaceful one. They are, in fact, monotonous in their repetition that an active, assertive child is a troublemaker and a quiet, quiescent, submissive, noncompetitive child is a good one.

Contrast may be made between child-training practices in the village and in the American middle class in regard to who may punish. That people in the village may physically punish a child not their own was sufficiently startling so that the custom was carefully checked. In effect, this increases the number of punishers to whom a child is subject. Anyone older than ego, regardless of sex or relation, is a socializer with powers of punishment. It has already been demonstrated that mothers will whip children who are not their own if they are fighting. But that is the point: the child's circle of disciplinarians is a circle, not a twosome. One mother expresses it this way, "Yes, X whips him too. Other people in the house also because they are all 'parents.' " Nonetheless, sanction from more distantly related kin is more likely to be verbal than physical. Parents do not resent the training their children receive from others. They do not designate it as interference and may express appreciation for it. In the middle-class American family the mother and father, or sometimes only one, are the only disciplinarians insofar as corporal punishment is concerned, although informal and less severe formal sanctions are wielded by many individuals.

If the Filipino child has many disciplinarians, he also has many who reward him. The larger circle of socializers means more people who may speak lovingly or approvingly to him and who give him privileges or items which are perceived as rewards. He may find sanctuary and condolence in many homes. The rewards investigated included approval shown by word or action, gifts, special privileges, and promises of something desirable. It is interesting to note that promises are defined for the child at a very early age as being merely words which may not and, in fact, probably will not, be observed. The child learns to interpret words as representing a pleasant verbal picture which seldom has any correlate in reality. Most middle-class American mothers are careful not to make a promise to a child which they could not keep and they emphasize to the child the importance of keeping his word. A major source of misunderstanding and conflict between Americans and Filipinos on a personal level is traceable to these contrasting customs. Filipinos are not disappointed when promises are not kept; that is what they have come to expect. They find Americans a trifle unreasonable in their insistence that words spoken in a promissory manner indicate that subsequent instrumental action will follow.

The striking differences in emphasis in child-training practices in the Philippines and America are due to differences between the cultures. Most important is that the Philippines is largely rural and agricultural, whereas America is largely urban and industrial. Other differences flow from these, between the family systems and perceptions of the empirical and nonempirical world. These differences are important and deserve a far more detailed narration than is suggested here, but such an inquiry is not the main focus of this study and shall have to await the dedication of future workers.

In this chapter we have been concerned with a number of topics. The first was kinship and kinship terminology. The bulk of the chapter was about mothers and children. Mother-child relationships were examined in the framework of these behavior systems: succorance, achievement, responsibility, obedience, sociability, dominance, and aggression. Separate subsections were devoted to forms of punishment and reward and a consideration of disciplinarians. Finally, the findings were discussed in relation to whether or not a given behavior system was emphasized or de-emphasized; whether the customary behavior was different for males and females; what differences were related to age; and, lastly, brief and intermittent comparison was made between the Filipino standards and those of middle-class American mothers. We now turn our attention from the mother-child dyad to woman-significant-other relationships.

Dyadic Relationships in the Family

THIS chapter is based on an analysis of dyadic role relationships from source material gathered in interviews. The interview was constructed in the field with two aims: the first, to collect focused, explicit material on the behavior customary between individuals in certain reciprocal social positions; the second, to structure such collected material in the framework of systems of behavior which had been previously formulated.[1]

Originally, the Whiting *Field Guide* had been drawn up to facilitate the study of socialization of the infant and child. I wanted to obtain information about the same variables in the behavior of adults. A schedule, outlined, tested, and revised several times, finally became the questionnaire presented in Appendix II. Each draft was discussed with an assistant, administered to a mother, and discussed again. In the course of pretesting, it became clear that information could not be elicited on all nine of the behavior systems. Six were adopted which proved most viable in constructing a formal interview. Participant observation and personal knowledge of the cultural configuration supplemented the material used in making the analyses.

On conclusion of the pretesting, twelve mothers were interviewed about their relationships with every member of their family of orientation and with their husbands.[2] The reciprocal positions investigated are husband, father, mother, older sister, younger sister, older brother, and younger brother. Mother-to-child relationships have already been described. Only one respondent had a member in every possible reciprocal position. Three could not remember a mother who died very young; the father of one had left the family when she was two; all had at least one sibling. The total number of dyads about which information was obtained was fifty-nine. Twelve men, unrelated to the mothers, were also interviewed about one or two dyadic relationships each, yielding information on an additional fifteen dyads. Data on three dyads in the in-law system were also obtained.

The following information came from women in the 25 to 48 age range, and from men age 26 to 70. The greater amount of information came from women. A word about the nature of the information based on childhood and contemporary orientation is in order. Oliver has spoken about two kinds of statements: the normative (shoulds and oughts); and the suppositional (cannot be reliably established; concerns past actions, unsupported opinions, and expectations about future actions).[3] Both kinds of statements may be found in the descriptions of dyadic relationship that follow. The normative are primarily concerned with present and recent situations, that is, the woman in her family today; the suppositional describes events from her childhood. It may be expected that when informants talk about their childhood roles, they are drawing more on memory and stereotype than when they recount contemporary incidents. It may also be expected that statements derived from the contemporary scene and those from childhood are differentially reliable.

Sometimes the interview was administered in the native dialect, Waray Waray, by my assistant. In a three-sided communication, the interpreter asked the questions in dialect and interpreted the answers to me, who recorded them in longhand and shorthand. I then considered whether the answer was relevant and specific and directed a probe, if necessary. While the questionnaire was administered in English to those mothers who were fluent in the language, the problems of limited understanding of bilinguals were not forgotten. After each question, the answer was considered. The assistant was trained to analyze with me whether or not the material offered was relevant to the inquiry. Sometimes it was necessary to repeat the question or probe to follow a promising line.

Soon after each interview the responses were typed for the files. During typing, there might be more discussion of the meaning of the women's answers, and the material they had offered was frequently supplemented by personal knowledge about the woman on the part of the assistant or the writer.

In both this and the preceding chapter, a categorization and definition of behavior systems formulated by Whiting *et al.*, have been of primary importance in ordering the data. In the mother-child relationships, the variables of succorance, achievement, responsibility, obedience, sociability, dominance, and aggression were studied. Some, though not all, are investigated here. Sociability and achievement are omitted because I could not devise questions to elicit satisfactory information on either. The difficulty with these two areas arose, I believe, for contrasting reasons. Achievement is not a valued behavior as is sociability, but the mechanics of sociability and the norms in which it functions are too complex to be uncovered in the simple interview system with which I worked. Two behavior systems were left out of the family relationship analysis and one not previously used was added. This was nurturance. Children were recipients of a good deal of nurturance but they were not necessarily and consciously trained to it. Nurturance, as an ideal, and as an attenuated practice, are part of adult life. The behavior systems to be discussed in this chapter have already been defined but for emphasis are restated below.

1. *Responsibility.* In any situation in which performance of an act, utterance of a phrase, or assumption of an attitude are clearly expected of ego, responsibility is the realization of the expectation. Responsibility consists of tendencies to be ready, willing and able to fulfill one's obligations, both implicit and explicit.

2. *Succorance.* Consists of tendencies to await or to signal for the nurturant response of another and to accept that response. Succorance is a state of dependency characteristic of infancy but also present in the growing and grown organism. When the organism is in tension a number of behaviors may be produced. Succorance is a behavior system in which predominant features are readiness for, and acceptance of, nurturance.

3. *Dominance.* Consists of tendencies to direct the acts of others and to enforce compliance and obedience in others. Dominance may be subtle or overt. One may attempt to direct another without making open or formal demands and one may consciously and autocratically seek to enforce one's will on others.

4. *Nurturance.* Consists of tendencies to respond to another so

as to lower tensions in the other. Need in the other may range from physical manifestations to mental phenomena or encompass both.

5. *Obedience.* In response to an initiation of action in others, obedience consists of tendencies to conform to hints, suggestions, requests, or demands that some course of action be carried out or some attitude be displayed. In situations in which obedience is involved, the other actor is acting dominantly. Nurturance is contrasted with obedience in that in the nurturant situation, the other actor is succorant, not dominant.

6. *Aggression.* Consists of tendencies to act with intent to hurt another. Aggression may be expressed in attitude, posture, speech, or action. Physical aggression is often only a small part of the gamut of possibilities. Aggression may be expressed by teasing, ridiculing, reprimanding, scolding, jeering, threatening, cursing, or otherwise abusing vocally.

DYADIC RELATIONSHIPS: PROCESSING

Two years after the field work, the dyadic relationship material was assembled for analysis. Processing the data continued at intervals for over a year, interrupted by teaching duties. The data were ordered both according to specific dyads (daughter-father, daughter-mother, or wife-husband) and to the behavior systems (nurturance, dominance, or aggression). While at first I analyzed the position of younger to older sibling separately from that of older to younger sibling for both sexes, the data eventually became so repetitive that only the positions of sister to brother and sister to sister were used in writing up the material. Special conditions relative to age subordination or superordination of a sibling were noted, however.

The system of processing involved abstracts and studies of all responses relevant to a particular dyad and to a particular system of behavior, and concluded with a descriptive and summary statement.

DYADIC RELATIONSHIPS:
FINDINGS — WIFE-TO-HUSBAND RESPONSIBILITY

The interview material reflected the primary concern of the people of Guinhangdan with economic matters and their keen consciousness of the vagaries and uncertainties of subsistence, especially in the statements of a wife's responsibility to her husband.

Securing food and the other necessities of living is a daily problem, and the responsibility of the wife in these matters touches on the entire range of procurement, preparation, distribution, and consumption. Transforming the produce of the field, sea, or market into edible condition is an important part of woman's role. Though some fruits are eaten raw, all meat, fish, rice, and most vegetables require preparation. The main cooking techniques are boiling and frying; roasting and sautéeing are reserved for ceremonial occasions, and there is no baking.

Although little in Philippine life calls for preplanning, serving food is one responsibility of some urgency. This no doubt reflects the periodic, sometimes continuous food shortage, and it also reflects the society's ideas about hunger. Wives are eagerly attentive to the mealtime needs of a husband who is a food producer, or — better still — a wage earner. The lazy or unemployed spouse does not fare so well. Meals ordinarily are served on the husband's arrival at the house or are sent out to him to the field or sea. Many decisions about when to do various kinds of work such as planting or harvesting are made according to the seasonal, daily, or ritual cycle. However, it is the responsibility of the wife to make many, if not most, of the nonrhythmical decisions. It is she who decides when nonseasonal crops shall be planted, preparation for a planting ceremony begun, or a propitiatory visit made to some relative whose plow or labor may be needed. The wife carries and doles out the money and has at least equal voice in decisions on purchasing; probably in many cases, she has greater decision-making power.[4]

While subsistence is a primary concern, the second most frequently mentioned responsibility is the care necessary in time of illness. All family members are mutually obligated to care for each other in time of illness. Because of the ubiquitousness of the responsibility, something of the nature of the obligation will be mentioned here and the responsibility for medical and nursing care will therefore not be elaborated in the dyads still to be described.

Etiology and treatment of illness is considered basically in supernatural terms. Reference to a pantheon of spirits and gods continues, although both natural causes and an embryonic understanding of micro-organismic causation are also part of native theory.[5] If the illness is serious enough, a curer may be summoned and the obligation for this payment falls on the family member who is able to meet it. Roots and leaves for poulticing, bathing, and drinking may be prescribed and family members sent to search for them. Nursing care includes sitting beside the patient, expressing concern about his temperature and comfort, procuring favorite foods, urging him to eat, and, perhaps, bathing him. Undoubtedly there is a rank order of sick care obligations to certain kin. I infer from general social structure, but do not know from direct questioning, that the order is parents first, spouse and children next, then siblings, and last, any other kin. It would be interesting to learn the choices of a series of individuals in given situations, if, for example, both mother and spouse were ill.

Significantly, illness modifies the behavior of any two individuals in a dyad. The invalid expects, and is permitted, a heightened amount of succorance. The caretaker is expected to be more nurturant than usual, in fact, the epitome in nurturance. The responsibilities of the invalid may diminish almost entirely, or, more commonly, are abrogated or temporarily ignored. The person who normally follows a conciliatory and obsequious behavior pattern is allowed greater directness and less ceremony when ill. Theoretically, though I do not have corroboratory information, the patient is permitted greater aggression.

The primary responsibilities of a wife to a husband, then, are procuring the daily necessities and providing care in time of illness. Other duties are far less prominent. Washing clothes in shallow tin pans with fluted edges is another responsibility of the women. Several women may work near a well, for a convenient water supply, or the chore may be performed in the home or yard. Clothes are ironed with a flatiron into whose hollow interior glowing charcoal is inserted.

A few wives feel responsibilities of temperament — that is, that a wife ought to be a balance for her husband's emotional state. If he is excited, she should remain calm; if he is phlegmatic, she should be a catalyst to movement. Only one woman mentioned a religious duty, namely, to urge her husband to practice being a good Catholic and to go to mass on Sunday. None mentioned sex.

Findings from the interviews with males about husbands' responsibilities emphasize the joint duties of husband and wife. A common answer is "to make plans with her on how to make a living." His first responsibility is subsistence maintenance; the second involves childbirth. When a woman delivers a child, her husband takes over the household — cooking, cleaning, laundry, care of any older children, and nursing care of the wife.

A woman is culturally sanctioned in foregoing her responsibilities if she is ill, in pain, has a great deal of work, is away from home, or less frequently, is sulking after a quarrel. The husband is excused from his responsibilities only if he is ill. Drunkenness is an explanation, but not an excuse, for not fulfilling responsibilities.

WIFE-TO-HUSBAND DOMINANCE

A wife asks her husband to do many household and occupational chores: gather fuel and hack it, go to the groves for coconuts, plant camotes, split bamboo, carry water, wash clothes, gather the nipa palm on the swampy shore, pound the hulls from rice, or repair a leaking roof or wall. The woman's domain is the home and the right to direct work is undisputed.

As soon as I wake up, I say "Where are you going now?" I tell the children to cook and do the errands and then I tell him, "All right, where are you going now? If you are going to the farm, start now."

I say, "Leave what you are doing and do this for me." If he is leaving the farm, I say, "You might as well wash the clothes first. Don't go away." To make him do it, I would sort of oil. I will talk in soft words. . . . If I want to force him I would say, "Faster, faster."

Most women couch their requests in a soft, low-spoken manner, using a technique to gain their ends which they translate as "oiling." In advertising terms, this is the soft sell, a technique which employs flattery and persuasion and a joking, pleasing-teasing remark. Such behavior is appropriate if the wife wants to buy some fish, have a special fruit when she is pregnant, buy a dress, or go to town for a movie. She asks her husband, wheedling and touching him lightly. If the husband resists the attempts at direction, the wife may let the matter drop, sulk, nag, remind him acridly of his duties, or she may act hurt and use withdrawal tactics — refuse to speak, leave the room, or threaten to leave the house.

He gives in most of the time because he wants to avoid trouble. When I am mad and don't speak to him, he speaks to me. I answer him harshly. Then our meals are unhappy and nobody wants to go to the table. If we have quarreled and I don't talk to him, at first he will leave me alone and then he will try to talk to me. I don't answer him.

Occasionally a wife may scold in a high-pitched voice, speak rapidly with controlled heat, or become openly angry and shout. In about two-thirds of the dyads collected, the women state that they persuaded the men by one technique or another. Tellingly, one said:

> I make him do it most of the time because he is my husband. I have to get him to do it for no one will do it for us. I don't want him to be the one telling me things. I am the woman.

and:

> Mostly I get him to do it because we are poor and have many children and if I don't get him to do it, we will have nothing to give to the children.

The age of the woman or her socioeconomic level does not change the pattern of dominance over her husband.

Lack of dominance of the husband is a strong theme in interviews with males:

> I give in most of the time because she is a woman and I feel sorry for her. I would not force her to do work.
> I give in most of the time because I cannot force her and it would only lead to trouble to try.

When asked what they would do if commanded by their wives to do something which they did not want to do, their responses were:

> Especially if I am a little bit tired, I say "I won't do it now but I'll do it in a few hours."
> I reason out, "In a minute. Give me a little rest. I will do it in a minute!"

WIFE-TO-HUSBAND SUCCORANCE

The pattern of displaying need and leaving the initiative of action to meet the need to another does not appear often in the responses of wives to questions about succorance or dominance. It may, of course, be used unconsciously. In many situations, I have observed that the appropriate behavior toward the person expressing need is remaining mute or propitiating feebly. In verbal reports, however, such technique does not appear common nor popular among the women.

WIFE-TO-HUSBAND NURTURANCE

If the husband is sad or unhappy, the wife questions him on the cause of his preoccupation. He may complain of the forgetfulness of children, quarrels, or the envy of other people. Sometimes husbands brood about poverty and their inability to buy certain things. Sometimes the wife becomes nurturant after causing the discontent, that is, after having refused him money to buy palm wine or to bet at the cockpit, she relents and gives him some.

The solicitous wife may do no more than ask a token question. She may joke or tease until the mood lifts; she may console by minimizing the importance of the cause. She is not necessarily always nurturant; she might quarrel with him if the mood is part of an ongoing disagreement. In any event, a mood of quietness in the husband calls for some response on the part of the wife, at least to the extent that she tries to find out what is wrong. Prolonged sulking, a technique used if other more pleasant techniques fail, requires that the other take note.

On the basis of data obtained, I am unable to determine a "normal" nurturing behavior in a wife. More in the nature of hypothesis than generalization, it can be said that nurturance is a valued, frequently mentioned ideal, although nurturant behavior is often not expressed both because of individual proclivities and because of the many frustrations inherent in daily life in this particular society.

WIFE-TO-HUSBAND OBEDIENCE

In daily life a husband often asks or tells a wife to go out and look for a certain kind of food, cook, or wash clothes. The wife complies if the request is softly and pleasantly worded and they have not been quarreling. If the husband tries to exact obedience to authoritative commands, he is acting in an unapproved manner and the wife may stare at him, ignore him, be elaborately sarcastic, or mimic him and start a quarrel. If the wife does not feel inclined to do whatever she is requested, in whatever manner the request is made, she may tell him to do it himself or ask one of the children to do it. Some wives feign illness but take care to make a good pretense of it. Spouses are adjured to be obedient to each other at the time of marriage. A husband reported: "Most of the time I obey her because that is the custom. Either party (husband or wife) would have to obey." The least we can say, then, is that an ideal of mutual obedience between husband and wife operates in the society.

WIFE-TO-HUSBAND AGGRESSION

A good deal of joking occurs in both daily and ceremonial life, and is supposed to be accepted in good part and with spontaneous laughter. Wives make jokes to their husbands most often on the subject of drinking palm wine. Women pretend that they will not give their husbands money or jokingly warn them that they will "get a big belly from drinking." The second most frequent source of jokes is the husband having a girl friend somewhere or meeting someone clandestinely. Personal performances are also the subject of jokes. For example, "When he was learning to dance, I say, 'You look like somebody who is paddling a boat. You don't look well. You don't know how to dance.' " The frailties of mankind come in for attention:

> For instance, if he dresses up to go to town, where he gets back he brags that he met somebody and they respected him because they thought that he was an authority or an official. I say in a mocking tone, sort of insulting, "Oh, yes, that's what he thought. He really thought you were an official. And that you were very handsome." He would laugh.

The difference between joking and teasing lies both in the intent of the jokes and the reaction of the target. If the wife intends only to provoke laughter she is joking, but if her intentions are to annoy, irritate, or anger, she is teasing. The distinction drawn is not categorical because prolonged joking tends to become teasing. In an ambivalent situation, the remark that is received by the husband with laughter is, therefore, a joke. In another ambivalent situation, the wife may intend to make a joke but the husband, through irritability, guilt, or enhanced sensitivity, takes it for teasing and gets angry. Men who have a reputation for being serious or hot tempered are teased less often. Only a little observation of Filipinos makes it apparent that teasing and joking are sanctions of pervasive influence.

Subjects about which husbands are teased, then, necessarily overlap with jokes. These include being given money for cockfighting or drinking, drinking too much, and staying overly long either with drinking cronies or at the cockpit. Having a fighting cock in the house or taking time to exercise a cock are also reasons for teasing. Teasing complaints are common when a husband's absence leaves the burden of baby and child care to the wife. He may be teased about a girl friend or a woman in town. The teasing is not all verbal. Sometimes it is a matter of manner. Women tease by touching lightly several times in a taunting manner, patting condescendingly, or throwing things at the other person in a provoking, feigned lighthearted manner.

When teasing becomes a reprimand, the lighthearted, make-believe element disappears. A sanction is being administered and nobody is in any doubt about it. The subjects about which husbands are reprimanded reflect both the greater importance of the behavior as contrasted to other behaviors and the loss of the playful element. The most common cause for reprimand is drinking and the second most common cause is leaving the home to go to town, neighbors, cockpit, gambling huts, or just to get away. The wife's irritation is increased if the husband has left tasks undone — rice unpounded, nipa uncut, or a child untended. Less commonly, a husband may be reprimanded for being irritable or speaking harshly to, or shouting at, the children.

A reprimand may be contrasted with scolding. A scolding lasts longer and is administered with more acrimony. The implication is that the target has repeated the offending action several times and needs, and deserves, to be spoken to at some length. The scolder has more reason to be angry and can afford to be a little less patient. Husbands are scolded by their wives for the same reasons that they are reprimanded, teased, or joked. In addition, failing to heed reprimands becomes cause for scolding. In other words, a sequence of more formal aggression may follow a series of less formal actions.

In summary, it may be said that wives tend to be responsible, dominant, and aggressive, rather than nurturant, succorant, or obedient.

DAUGHTER-TO-FATHER RESPONSIBILITY

The general tone of a daughter-to-father relationship is one of respect and obedience. In some cases, this is tinged with fear, but more often the relationship is warm and affectionate. A gesture of obeisance, known as "kissing the hand," is accorded both parents on certain occasions, which is illustrative. Offspring, both male and female, child and adult, kneel before a parent and hold his or her hand to the forehead. Actually, there is no kissing. Obeisance is observed after the Angelus bell has rung in the evening, on the return home after Sunday Mass, before leaving home on a lengthy journey, or on coming into the parent's presence in the evening without having performed the gesture that day.

A daughter's responsibility to a father is more pronounced and binding while she is growing up or still living at home than after her marriage. However, her duties as a caretaker of her father are the core of her role to him, both when she is in her family of orientation and in her family of procreation. She should serve him food when he returns from the fields or sea, run any errands he requests or orders, wash and iron his clothes, take care of him when he is ill, and be respectful and cheerful. In later years, she should help him financially, particularly when he is observing a fiesta, or sponsoring a baptism, marriage, or memorial service. The eldest daughter occupies a special position. If her mother dies she must look more fully after her father's well-being. She may accompany him to town or on visits when normally the mother would have done so. The youngest daughter appears to be the most indulged; she may complain and accuse the parent in ways the other children cannot; she also is less frequently punished and her misdemeanors are tolerated longer.

Any time that the daughter is home she is at the beck and call of the father. Marriage and, ultimately, setting up her own residence, frees her somewhat from service responsibilities. A separate residence makes it more difficult for the father to request services and easier for the daughter to plead responsibilities in her own home, particularly when her family begins to grow. Nonetheless, daughters assume considerable responsibility for their fathers. The only excuse for nonperformance at any age (outside of pressure of responsibilities of one's family of procreation in later life) is sickness and pain.

DAUGHTER-TO-FATHER DOMINANCE

If the father is unwilling or unable to concur with a daughter's request, she may desist but she will usually pursue the matter a little. She may coax or wheedle or, in the event that she is a favorite of his, cry, or refuse to eat. Openly coercive techniques are more common while the female is a child, and virtually disappear in the adult, but one mature daughter, an unusually dominant woman, blatantly displays anger at her father and is not above dropping a few plates to make a point. While many attempts are made, more or less subtly, to direct father's actions, few attempts are overtly made to dominate or force him. "It is very improper for me to force him because he is my father." It is assumed that father will "give" if he possibly can; if he refuses, it is probably because he is physically or financially unable to do so.

DAUGHTER-TO-FATHER SUCCORANCE

When a daughter wants her father to do something for her, such as lifting a can of water, making a toy, buying fried bananas or a dress, climbing a tree for young coconuts, cutting down a banana tree, killing a chicken, or doing some farm work, she asks slowly, using a low, pleading tone. She may touch him lightly, put her arms around his shoulders, stroke him, say "father, father," smile at him, promise to do some work for him, or buy him some palm wine to put him in a good mood. She uses conciliatory and propitiatory techniques. In the absence of her husband, a woman often seeks the aid of her father in tasks that are beyond her strength or ability.

DAUGHTER-TO-FATHER NURTURANCE

The daughter may be expected to help the father obtain the family's material needs, go to market, fetch water, cook, write a letter, and aid him with physical tasks in his declining years, all in a cheerful nurturant manner. According to cultural ideal, grown children must enjoin their parents not to undertake the heavier tasks and, whenever possible, to do it for them, or they will be the subject of gossip. Significantly, elderly parents are not unqualifiedly nurtured where the food supply is concerned. It is a cultural ideal that the old folks will not eat or want as much as the younger ones. This attitude serves as a thin veil over the fact that the food supply is not plentiful, often insufficient, and that those who are supposed to do without are the elderly nonproducers.

However, if a father sits brooding, sad, or unhappy, most daughters seek to find the reason for his distress and to provide some consolation. A few fear a punitive father and leave him alone, but usually they will inquire into the cause of the mood, sitting beside him, touching him, and coaxing him to confide in them. Fathers are saddened by the disobedience of children, quarrels with familial members and others, and the pressing need for money. The daughter may give him money, offer him food, perform the neglected chore herself, urge him to pay no attention to the matter, or make a joke of the whole thing. She seeks to dispel his bad mood.

If the father is sick and the mother feeble or absent, the daughter takes care of the father, sees that he has clean clothes, cooked food, and nursing care. Children bear a strong obligation to care for a feeble or ill parent. It is explained that it would be a shame for a nonfamilial member to assume the responsibility, that the child feels pity and compassion for the parent, and that one should repay the care and sacrifice the parent has given.

DAUGHTER-TO-FATHER OBEDIENCE

During childhood and girlhood, a daughter is often bidden by her father to perform various household or field chores: feeding the animals, gathering fuel, pounding rice, or fetching water. Most of the time the daughter obeys the father because obedience is an ideal, because she may fear punishment, or because of the strong theme of reciprocity in the culture. "I obey most of the time because anything I request him to do, he would also do." However, various delays and evasions are practiced by the daughter. If she is unwilling to comply, she may plead that she must care for the baby. "I would pick up a younger sibling into my arms and pretend to be rocking the baby." She may pretend to be ill or in pain. Sometimes a daughter procrastinates, saying, "Wait a minute, wait a minute," until the need for the chore is past. Occasionally, a girl makes an open refusal tempered by the suggestion that another child do the task. Or a girl may plead, "Mother told me to do something else." Despite numerous procrastinations (more are yet to be described), normally both young and grown children are ultimately if not immediately obedient.

DAUGHTER-TO-FATHER AGGRESSION

Joking situations based on false information are commonplace in many societies. In our own, a child may be sent to buy striped paint, or a novice sent for a left-handed monkey wrench or a bucket of steam. Being sent on a fool's errand is part of village joking. Joking situations are sometimes initiated by a daughter, who might say, "Father, you are invited to go drinking in their house," when, as a matter of fact, they either are not drinking or have not invited him. She may pretend to have been unable to get something he wanted from town, or enters the house claiming to have killed a chicken. Father may be mimicked gently or be the subject of jokes for his attempt to speak another dialect. A common theme about which a daughter jokes with a father is remarriage, even if the mother is still alive, although usually when the father is a widower.

As we have said, teasing is joking carried on until the target becomes angry. A daughter will tease her father most frequently with disobedience and noncompliance. She may put off complying with a request until the father gets angry, then say she was only teasing. "If he told me to do something, I would be reluctant and delay and say, 'Ah, I will not go there,' and he would insist and I would say again, 'Ah, I will not go there.' He is already mad and I would do it." Or, if, on returning late from town, she treats his concern lightly and he becomes angry, she may say she was only teasing. Or she may openly refuse to obey, telling herself she is only teasing and will obey the order eventually, or she may hide when called.

Not all daughters tease their fathers. Some fathers are too feared or respected to make this relationship possible, but most daughters do tease. It is immediately obvious that the subjects about which they tease are strain points in their relationships, for the demands on Filipino children for obedience are quite onerous. Some of the burden of learning obedience and of being obedient is alleviated through joking — by making fun of being less obedient, or by making a joke of temporary disobedience. Other subjects of teasing are old age, old people eating more than they need by cultural prescription, drinking, remarriage, and money.

A daughter may reprimand her father for drinking, gambling, staying away from home for a prolonged period, quarreling with mother, being irritable or bad-tempered, using strong language, or speaking harshly to younger siblings. Conversely, the father may be reprimanded for doing errands which he might have delegated to his children or for undertaking tasks which are too heavy for the aged.

A daughter does not scold her father. This is outside the range of permissible actions. She may give advice and suggestions, joke, tease, or reprimand, but she would not scold for fear of punishment, both physical and supernatural. The omnipotent Deity looks upon such action as dishonoring parents.

In summary, daughters tend to be respectful to fathers and to assume and maintain many responsibilities toward them. Efforts to dominate a father must be muted and brief. The three systems, succorance, nurturance, and obedience are all emphasized in the daughter-father relationship. Finally, daughters are limited in the aggression they may direct toward fathers.

DAUGHTER-TO-MOTHER RESPONSIBILITY

The primary duties of a daughter to a mother are to care for and help her in all ways and to be respectful and obedient. As a mere toddler, a little girl plays at the household chores which will later form a considerable part of her responsibilities to her family. A daughter helps with care of the clothes and preparation of the food and her contribution to household maintenance is considerable. Nonetheless, she acts with humility, frequently seeking advice and instruction from the parent and almost always awaiting direction. As an adolescent or young woman, the daughter may have financial resources either as a wage earner or as a wife; she then aids her mother financially. An unmarried woman gives all her earnings to her mother. The daughter is not considered to have any personal right to her earnings. If she desires something, she solicits it in the same manner as does a nonwage earner.

Expectation closely approximates the ideal — that all her life a daughter will give financial and moral support to her mother in whatever measure she can. If her mother is young and still bearing children, a daughter will help to care for her at delivery and take considerable responsibility for the younger siblings. When a daughter is away from home, and whether she is married or not, she returns at times of crisis in the maternal home. In the event of a death in the family the daughter returns to comfort the mother; at the memorial services she seeks someone to lead the prayers; she helps with the household work. In times of sickness, the daughter nurses the mother, perhaps moving her to her own household to do so. In her mother's old age, she may assume a substantial part of the responsibility of food procurement for her. If they maintain separate households, the daughter often sends food or supplies to her.

Only a few reasons and a few occasions free a daughter from her responsibilities to a mother. These are the times of her own childbearing, illness, and, rarely, the pressure of her own work. Most commonly, the mother's requests come first. If the household of the daughter is some distance from that of the mother, she is called upon less frequently.

DAUGHTER-TO-MOTHER DOMINANCE

As I have already indicated in the father-daughter dyad, dominant behavior of a child to a parent is not encouraged. Attempts at direction are covert and the women are unconscious that they are making any efforts at dominance. As adults, women flatter and bribe a mother; as children and adolescents, though rarely as adults, they may cry to attain their ends. These actions are not understood as attempts at direction and enforcement. "I do not command her. I only request her."

If daughters do not think of themselves as attempting dominance over their mothers, it is also true that they rarely make open and sustained attempts at direction. A number of valid reasons explain such behavior. The following include reasons which they can verbalize. An attempt to dominate on the part of a child stands in opposition to an important moral and religious injunction: "Be ye obedient and respectful to elders," especially to parents. Furthermore, as already has been noted, family figures are stereotypes: mothers are regarded as completely loving and indulgent beings who will do everything possible for the care and comfort of their young. Ideally, such care is given unsolicited. If, however, a female child is in need, the most forward actions permissible are low-level pressures. Examples:

At first, I tell her stories and smile at her and then afterwards when she is in a good mood, I request, "Inay, will you please go to so and so's house and request this? I am ashamed to go there." Like requesting money from a neighbor because our pension hasn't come yet and we will give percentage. She always did it. Sometimes I stroke her hair or pat her or put my arms around her shoulders.

Another example is getting her to stay with the children when I go away. "Inay, watch the children for me for we are going out. We won't be gone long." I talk to her in pleading tones and I say, "When we come back, we will bring things to you."

To sum up, the more overt, direct, and visible techniques of dominance are completely outside the range of permissible behaviors of a daughter to a mother; the muted ones have a limited expression.

DAUGHTER-TO-MOTHER SUCCORANCE

Conversely, a woman in a daughter role emphasizes succorance. The approved techniques for seeking nurturance from a mother as an adult include a simple, polite, direct request with no follow-up, and other more elaborate measures. The latter are illustrated below:

If the pension arrives and I am asking money, I say "Please give me some money." She says, "Don't ask now. Next time." I oil. I go with her to cash the check. I sit beside her and pluck at her arm.

If she has something I admire, I say, "Are you using this? I like it very much." She says, "All right, you can have it." There was a framed saint I wanted very much. I loved that picture. I asked her for it and she gave it to me. I oil by stroking her and I ask her over for palm wine and that is when I would ask.

A woman in her adult years is most likely to be seeking food, money, or help in care of the children. Although some individuals seek more help than others and thus lessen the effect of their actions, most requests are based on genuine need, voiced only when the need is pressing, and such a condition carries a compelling force to a people who know it well.

If, after the daughter has signaled her need and seen the signal register with the mother, her request is not met, several types of withdrawal behavior are common: she may act hurt, not speak for several hours, or refuse to eat. Although withdrawal behavior is most common, one woman reported using the constant low-intensity pressures of beseeching tones and repeated entreaties until she achieved her purpose. But, for the most part, it is considered improper and unseemly to attempt to beg, tease, or nag a mother into an attitude or action to aid one. A very few daughters make pretenses of illness to escape an onerous duty, but such pretenses cannot be indefinitely maintained. The obligation of obedience to mother is stronger than that to husband. "I am forced to do it because she is my mother. I don't make pretenses with her like with my husband."

Obedience to elders is a value in his village society and the rationale offered for the frequency and range of behavior is that: It is duty; one has an obligation to take care of the caretaker who raised one; "it is natural" to obey one's mother; and love makes one obedient.

DAUGHTER-TO-MOTHER AGGRESSION

A daughter makes jokes to her mother on a variety of subjects. First, she will often give false information — that the mother is needed somewhere when she is not, or that a child is hurt when he is not. Then, she may make a joking pretense that mother is beautiful when both really know that she is not. Sometimes, a daughter has been unsuccessful in seeking some favor or article and her pretended disobedience that follows is classed as a joke. Again, a mother may request that her daughter delouse her or pick out the white hairs and the daughter will twist her hair into little braids instead. Less playful, but still defined as joking, are remarks about old people who should not feel hunger but do, and the possible loss of a family member through marriage.

More of a tease than a joker is the daughter who, after her mother had drunk palm wine, slept and awakened, addressed her with concealed sarcasm, "Go ahead mother, drink some more. You will be singing and making speeches." Joking behavior can become teasing behavior in time if the joke is repeated often enough. One daughter used the same joking theme to tease until it angered her mother. The daughter asked the mother for money and on being refused made playful accusations that the parents were buying things they did not need, thus depriving her. Prolonged disobedience in a teasing manner may also cause aggression. Another touchy subject is a widowed mother's remarriage.

She was a widow. If a single old man walked by I say, "Inay, you better get married, you have no husband," and she would laugh at us. She got mad if I insisted, "Inay, get married. You don't want to live with us. You have no child in the house. Better get married." She got mad. She would say, "All right, if you don't want to take care of me, all right."

What the daughter has to say about her own marriage is also illustrative of the strain involved in family reorganization when a member leaves or enters.

When I was still single I would say, "Oh, I am going to get married." She would get mad. They don't want us to get married because then we are not around to do errands and help.

A daughter may reprimand a mother on any subject concerning the latter's nonconformance to certain behavioral ideals. For instance, it is incumbent upon offspring to care for parents in their old age and, to lighten their work and dispel their worry in every way possible. When the old people do not play the complementary role of dependency with little or no initiative and show too much self-responsibility, they are likely to be reproved by their offspring. Daughters may chide mothers about undertaking tasks which are heavy for aging muscles: carrying fuel, harvesting, or polishing floors. The way a mother spends money and the severity or inappropriateness of punishment of the children on her part are also subjects of reprimand.

During meals she would scold my younger brothers and I would reprimand her for scolding during meal time. Also for whipping the children when she is in her temper. She would knock their heads.

The ideal personality type for mature females is a cheerful, non-aggressive, unconcerned kind of person. Contrary types are criticized:

She is touchy; she gets hurt easily. I reprimand her for that. If she gets disappointed with one of my sisters, she keeps on thinking deep thoughts and I reprimand her, "Don't be like that. It will ruin your health when you think so much. Be cheerful. Come on, let's drink some palm wine."

Mothers may be scolded but this does not happen very often. To so treat a mother is to dishonor her and run the risk of censure from fellow villagers and the Deity. However, occasionally a mother is scolded for being too easygoing and generous; perhaps for giving away precious supplies of rice to the needy, or for giving too freely of the scant family supplies to a favorite child so that the others have less. In effect, she is scolded for certain virtues and the scolding cannot be wholehearted.

In summary, a daughter has many lifelong responsibilities to her mother. She does not attempt much dominance but she is highly succorant. The ideal of nurturing the mother is often realized. Daughters are highly obedient and low in aggression to mothers.

SISTER-TO-SISTER RESPONSIBILITY

An older sister is treated with respect similar in many ways to that accorded a parent. This respect is given even if the age gap between the pair is only one year. The special position held by the older or oldest sister within the family is attested by the fact that some younger sisters call their older sisters by the maternal term of address, *nanay*. This practice is more common in childhood than in later years and occurs only in a restricted number of families. Performing the obeisance of kneeling to an older sister when one is a child, as well as when there are marked age differences between the sisters, is another infrequent practice but one that does occur and reflects the special responsibilities and privileges of the older sister. A younger sister asks permission of an older sister, in the same manner as she would ask her parents, to leave the house and visit with her friends. In the event of the mother's death, the older sister will assume many of the responsibilities of the mother and the younger sister will increase her respect accordingly.

A sister has responsibilities to teach, watch over, and guide a younger sister. She advises on practical matters and supervises her younger sibling. Her advice should be sought and accepted. She imprints the homely truths upon her younger siblings, telling them not to be quarrelsome or lazy, to respect elders, and to help them at all times. Elder sister is a reservoir of knowledge not only about how elders should be treated but about how they have met and solved the recurrent problems of life. Younger sister has the responsibility of helping elder sister in all aspects of daily household routine and child care.

Sisters help each other in times of illness, death, childbirth, or baptism. One crisis rite in which their responsibilities to each other are minimal is marriage for, at this time, it is the duty of the groom's family to provide money, food, labor, and orators.

SISTER-TO-SISTER DOMINANCE

Virtually no expression of dominance to an older sister occurs, but repeated attempts at dominance of a younger sister are the rule. Of course, girls and women vary individually in the degree of dominance which they attempt over younger sisters. They may argue, shout, or threaten to tattle to mother, whose authority is not to be gainsaid.

I get mad and say, "How hardheaded you are. What I am telling you to do is not hard, still you don't want to do it." I force her by talking.

The statement "if I always force, she won't do it any more," indicates that there are limits on the amount of dominance possible.

The examples of elder sisters' dominance encompassed household and child care and personal service. Initially in a soft voice, a sister asks a younger sister to go to the store for her, to shred some coconut, or to mind the baby. If the younger does not heed, after a few repetitions of the request, she may be reminded that she also will want things done for her. The reciprocity theme is important. Much dominance is verbal. Another telling example:

I would say harshly, "Go ahead and do it," and she would say, "In a minute," and I would say loudly, "All in a minute. All in a minute."

Several women rationalized the directing of their sisters by saying that they were performing a service to them; they were training them in the daily necessities of life. If they felt an explanation was necessary, they might add, "I get her to do it so that I can finish my work." However, the younger is not entirely without recourse for refusal. The press of her own work, illness, or childbirth are sufficient reasons for not helping the older sister. She may appeal to the parents if she feels she is being treated with too much direction and, perhaps, unjustly.

SISTER-TO-SISTER SUCCORANCE

When a younger sister seeks a favor from an older sister, she waits for a propitious time. If the latter is occupied, the younger will not make her needs known; but if the older sister is free, the younger will address her in a humble, supplicatory manner and speak slowly, softly, and pleadingly. She may smile, coax, and put her arms around her sister's shoulders. She may ask for money, firewood, cooked food, or raw fruit or vegetables, or ask her sister to mind her children. She may wish to borrow a dress. In general, the items or services requested are minor.

If an older sister refuses a succorant request, a younger sister may withdraw or sulk. "Sometimes I get hurt and say in an aggrieved tone, 'It's all right if you don't want to give.' And she would buy." Rather rarely, one might cry in an attempt to persuade an older sibling. A more common response is to withdraw and refuse to speak. There is no nagging or outright attempt at coercion, for such techniques are incompatible with the respect orientation incumbent upon the younger sister. Most older sisters comply with the request of the younger ones, partly because the younger ones are circumspect about what and how they ask, and partly because it is the well-learned duty of the elder to help. But it is plain that the preferred mode of expression for younger sister to older sister is succorance, not dominance.

A younger sister may be frequently and successfully succorant to the elder because of age, achievement, or possession of goods. Succorance in the elder cannot be explained in the same way. The elder also frequently expresses needs to the younger which it is incumbent upon the latter to meet. For the most part, such needs seem to be minor in nature and are more common in childhood, for example, pleas to receive a delicacy or a few centavos which the younger received in a recent windfall. In adulthood, food and money may still be sought of the younger, but in more substantial amounts.

The older sister pleads, uses an affectionate nickname, flatters, cajoles, caresses. Again, as illustrated in the dominance expression, the rationale of training enters. "I get her to give to me so that she will not be trained to be greedy." Generosity is an inculcated virtue. "She hates to be called greedy."

SISTER-TO-SISTER NURTURANCE

One may help an older sister by minding her children, cooking, or helping her with money-producing tasks like sewing nipa, but the most frequently mentioned form of nurturance is nursing in times of illness. Younger sister may also perform errands, such as seeking an outrigger canoe which elder sister may borrow to go out to the fields up the river. When they are children together, a sister will watch over younger sister protectively, seeing that she does not play too far from the house or fall from the ladder stairways. The elder sister may be the one to prepare and serve food to her school child sister. If the youngster is ill, she will sit beside her, coaxing her to eat and giving her toys that please her.

Among the events which may sadden an older sister are quarrels with her husband or other family members, a scolding from her father or mother, or failure on the part of someone to lend her money. The cheering up process is described as follows: a younger sister approaches the brooder calmly with real or simulated good spirits. She asks questions to find the cause of the misery, then advises her how to attain peace and harmony once again. She may lend her money or console her verbally, saying, "Never mind," "Leave it alone," or "Are you sure that what you are worried about is true?" Younger sisters are petulant, sulky, or weepingly unhappy for a number of reasons: quarreling or fighting with another child, a quarrel with a family member, or the refusal of a parent to give money to purchase something. The older sister consoles her, sometimes backing her up in a quarrel with another child not of the family, or giving her money if she can. In view of the ideals of nonaggression, two sisters' advice to discomforted younger sisters is rather surprising.

I say, "What's the matter with you? Did somebody quarrel with you? Let's go there. We will take revenge." We would go there and throw sand and stones at them. Then we would run back home quickly.

I keep on asking her, "What's the matter? Why are you crying?" And she will say, "I was passing by the neighbor's house and the child there pushed me and hit me right away. I didn't even touch her." I will tell her, "Stop crying. If she will pass by this afternoon or any time, you hit her."

In this instance, aggression to somebody outside of the dyad under study constitutes nurturance to one of the members within it.

SISTER-TO-SISTER OBEDIENCE

A younger sister is highly obedient to an older sister. A suggestion or order from the elder has the weight of a command from a parent and is seldom disobeyed. A younger sister may occasionally procrastinate a little, seek someone (her own children, perhaps) to fulfill the command for her, or pretend illness. A strong sense of duty, love, and the importance of reciprocity are primary motivating factors in younger sister's obedience to older sister.

Younger sisters cannot, with impunity, attempt to command elder sisters. They are generally limited to making requests.

How dare you command an elder! You can do it yourself, why not do it. You can see how busy I am. It really shows how bad your character is. . . . It is improper for a younger sister to command an elder. If I do anything she commands me, she will get used to be commanding and there will be a time when she will abuse and will do it to our parents.

I would say, "Oy, don't command me, I'm not your servant. Bah! You pretend to be a mother. Don't be commanding me. You are not a mother. . . ." But if it is a request and she does it in a soft way, I'd do it.

A younger sister will be scolded if her request is too peremptory. One atypical younger sister exercised unusual influence and control over her sister, but the circumstances that made this possible were also unusual. The younger had outstanding status; she was a teacher, a landowner, owner of a store, and, in general, a power to be reckoned with in the community. When the situation is reversed and younger sister is markedly lower in the social scale than older sister, the servitude of the younger is increased. For instance, one woman, whose older sister is married to a judge and whose status is therefore high, is often called upon to perform menial tasks which are normally left to children.

SISTER-TO-SISTER AGGRESSION

A good bit of teasing among children who are sisters revolves around property such as toys, clothes, or money. An elder sister may threaten to hide the shell game of a younger; she may accuse her of stealing money and keep up the pretense until the younger cries. What is one's temporary property such as a plate at a meal may be snatched and hidden when the user's head is turned. In addition to threats against property, some privilege may be threatened, or fears aroused: "The asuang will get you!"

By this time it may be expected that when respect and obedience comprise the ideal forms of expression in a relationship, the amount and kind of aggression permitted will be minimized. Younger sisters mentioned several subjects about which they joked and teased their older sisters. Brothers-in-law may be the subject.

For instance, I say, "Mana, I saw your husband with another woman. They were going together, talking and laughing." She would say, "Never mind him. It's better if he will bring another woman home so that I will have a helper at home."

For instance I would say, "Isang, does your husband ever caress you or make romance with you now that you are already old?"

The theme of false information giving recurs. "Your husband just got off the bus." "When I was visiting her in Dumaguete, I would joke that I was going back to Leyte right away." Or, an older sister may be joked about singing offkey or speaking in another dialect.

It is interesting to note that sister's dogs and children may be scapegoats and to such helpless targets, aggression may be more direct.

[I tease her . . .] by teasing her child and making him cry. Sometimes I would pinch him. Also if the child asked for food and I didn't give it.

One time she had a pet dog. It got sick with a skin disease: the hair came out. It was her favorite. Sometimes I would kick it and say, "Why are you letting this dog stay with you? It has a disease. You might get sick." And she would get mad because it is her pet.

Disinclination to obey an older sister's commands may be handled with a joke on younger sister's part.

When she tells me to do something, I would refuse at first. Then she will insist and I also insist refusing. Then she gets mad and I would say,

"All right. I'll do it. I just wanted to see your face how you look when you are mad."

A younger sister may reprimand an older sister within a limited area of social relations. Almost every woman mentioned sisters' quarrels with husbands as legitimate cause for reprimands. Younger sisters have a definite stake in the harmony of sister's family of procreation. In the same vein, a sister's harshness to her children is cause for rebuke. Any action which threatens the peace of the family is potentially disruptive and sufficient cause for the younger to rebuke the older about it. An interesting sidelight is that reprimands are not always directed against the acts themselves, but often because they may attract unfavorable neighborly attention.

Also when she scolds with a very big voice, "Why can you not scold, Nana, without a very big voice. Everyone will know you are scolding because you are roaring like a lion. Why don't you pinch each other in the bedroom without roaring."

The underlying rationale for limited aggression against elder sister have been mentioned before: they are respected; it is duty; and God's punishment is feared.

When we consider sister-to-younger-sister aggression, we again find a marked interest in sister's spouse. An example concerning the food supply and obligations to share follows:

When her husband has just come home from fishing and I'd ask her if he was able to catch many fish, she would answer, "None." Then I'd joke and say, "Even if there are plenty, you still say none."

The implication in a joke about food and one's familial obligation may be more clearly drawn:

When she insists on saying that her husband could not catch many fish, then I would also insist, saying, "I saw him carrying many fish and I was even informed that he was able to sell much." Then she would get mad if I insist on teasing her.

A younger sister may make jokes to her older unmarried sister about her boy friends or her appearance.

A younger sister may be reprimanded about many things — for scolding or quarreling with a younger sibling, nagging or quarreling with her husband, endangering herself climbing coconut trees or going on the river, or for carelessness in work. Apparently, younger sister imitates the elder sister by teasing yet younger siblings, but she is not allowed as much aggression. A hierarchy of permissible responses definitely accrues the advantages to the older.

Concern about health is mirrored in what a younger sister may be scolded about — washing her feet or getting wet when she is menstruating. What she allows her children to do may bring this reaction from an older sister:

> I would scold her when she permits her children to go to the river bank by themselves. I fear that they might get drowned if they happen to go to the water. So I would scold her for tolerating [allowing] them.

Disobedience, procrastination, or avoidance may elicit this response:

> She goes out a lot and I scold her especially if I am tired of the work and I have to cook, look for fuel, fetch water, and take care of the baby alone.

In summary, it may be said that girls and women tend to be responsible both to younger and older female siblings; that older sisters tend to dominate younger sisters; that younger sisters tend to be obedient and seldom, if ever, attempt to command older sisters; that sisters are mutually succorant and nurturant, regardless of who is the junior; and that considerable aggression is permitted an older sister and considerably less aggression is tolerated in a younger sister.

SISTER-TO-BROTHER RESPONSIBILITY

The diffuse authority which parents and an older sister maintain is also shared by an older brother. A girl is expected to be respectful, helpful, and obedient to him. She speaks circumspectly, runs errands, helps him to achieve a good personal appearance at times when a little display is necessary, as when he is courting, seeking a job, or visiting. Since he is an elder, he is yet another person from whom she should seek advice and accept guidance.

However, her obligations to him are less rigid than those to parents, spouse, or female siblings, and the circumstances that excuse her from meeting them are increased. Sickness or pain free her, but so, too, do less urgent contingencies, such as being scolded by him in public or having had a fight with him. Such personal circumstances, freeing a person from obligations, were of minor significance in other dyads.

The stream of responsibility is reversed toward a younger brother. A sister takes care of a younger male sibling in his childhood years, seeing to it that he has clean clothes for school and other important occasions. Just as she is advised by elders, so she advises him to be respectful and to do the things that elders tell him to do. She frequently reprimands, admonishes, guides, and coaxes him.

As boys become adolescents and young bachelors, both younger and older sisters assume new responsibilities and concerns for them. Economically and socially, a new role for the maturing males is imminent. This role is foreshadowed by their increasing attraction to, and attention to, the peer group and by their visits to the plaza, other villages, towns, feasts, and dances. This is the age at which young males begin to imbibe palm wine and sister now adds strictures about drinking and drinking companions to her admonitions. But the main reason why a girl's responsibilities to her brother come into focus at this time is because boys in the family are especially dependent on females during courtship and at the time of their marriage. It is customary for the boy's family to bring food and orators to the girl's home. There they prepare a feast and serve it, while their orators attempt to persuade the girl's people of the felicity of the match. The ceremony entails considerable financial cost and labor. A sister helps both at the marriage arrangement meetings and at the nuptials proper.

SISTER-TO-BROTHER DOMINANCE

During childhood, a sister may send her brother to the store for fish, rice, oil, or lard. She may direct him in many chores which are compatible with his age and strength. Both as a child and as an adult, he is called upon to help her by lifting and carrying heavy things such as a sack of rice, big utensils, coconuts, or large containers of water. When the sister is married, she might, in the temporary absence of her husband, seek his aid in performing certain chores such as chopping wood, cutting and splitting bamboo stalks for nipa sewing, retrieving coconuts from the tall palms, or doing repair work. Since more latitude exists for independent action and reaction in a sibling relationship than in a parent-child relationship, these attempts at direction of the action of another can be expected to be accompanied by a certain obsequiousness and a full use of flattery. The following quotation documents a different orientation to husband and brother in regard to dominance. "A brother is different from a husband. We can't make them do something immediately"; but the remark also implies that brothers are dominated.

If the age difference between the two is marked, as in the case of one woman whose brother is twelve years older, her attempts to control him are strongly influenced by the age factor. She is less direct in approach, takes care to talk softly, to flatter and entertain him beforehand, and may preface her attempt with a gift of palm wine. However, indirection is not necessarily the rule. In general, a woman's request of her brother is forthrightly stated, and is recognized by some women as being more in nature of a command. Nonetheless, the age factor cannot be overlooked. Another factor, important in individual cases, involves the brother's indebtedness to the sister for past favors received or anticipation of her help in forthcoming ceremonies. Such dependence on her makes him more compliant.

If a brother is unwilling to comply with attempts at direction he may be coaxed, cajoled, flattered, or coerced in some way.

I get hurt and don't talk to him. If we are going to meet on a path, I turn away and find another way. This only lasts a few hours. I force by harsh tones and stamping my feet.

When they are still children, she may whip him around the legs with the midrib broom, either playfully or in earnest. However, open dominance is more in order to younger brothers than to older brothers. No woman fails to pay lip service to the cultural ideal of nonforcing elder brothers. They will say, "I do not force him. He is my older brother. That would not be respectful." Nevertheless, the evidence points to a high degree of attempts at dominance both to older and younger brothers, despite the added possibility that some sisters may be afraid of physical violence should elder brother be too provoked.

A brother who is truly unwilling and who refuses direction shows his attitude by ignoring the directive, not looking at his sister, and leaving the room or vicinity. The frequency with which brothers comply seems to depend in part on the need of the sister. If she has tasks which no one else can do for her, she will persist until he helps her. If the matter is optional, or there is some alternative in who shall perform the task, she may give up when he shows reluctance. In minor matters, he may perform one small chore and avoid further duty by escaping from her voice and presence. Independent personal traits also enter. Some individuals are categorized as being "so stubborn that you cannot get them to do anything."

It might seem, on the face of it, that greater attempts of dominance on the part of the women occur when siblings are both youngsters or adolescents. But the pattern persists throughout adult life, even when the women have their own families and are no longer resident with the family of orientation.

In regard to the sister-older brother relationship, it is interesting to note that the more secure a woman is and the more warm and spontaneous the relationship, the easier it is for her to seek his aid without preliminaries and without recourse to mild deceptions and seductions. The greater the age differential between them and the more the relationship between them includes a component of respect and avoidance, the greater the compulsion she is under to make a ritual out of her attempts at dominance and the more time and effort she must put into it. But this is part of the larger, over-all sister-to-older brother relationship which, in some cases, is so like the parent-child relationship that it includes the respect obeisance of kneeling at Angelus.

SISTER-TO-BROTHER SUCCORANCE

Many acts which are defined as attempts at dominance become acts of succorance when viewed in another perspective. I am aware that these shadings of meaning constitute a controversial aspect of the systems of behavior. The difference lies in the intent and manner of the actor. Thus, if a woman merely signals her need, or passively waits for help, she is succorant, whereas, if she takes direct action to achieve compliance, she is being dominant. The distinction is not always easy to make. The difficulty arises when one attempts to designate the point at which a plea for succorance becomes an attempt at dominance. Of course, nagging can transform a previously succorant attitude into attempts at dominance, yet subtleties of interaction are involved which are not always easy, or even possible, to discern with any certainty.

When they are children, a sister asks a brother for help with many aspects of manual labor, such as getting water or fuel or hauling coconuts. When they are grown, she is apt to ask him for money, food, or some minor service. The method of asking does not seem to be patterned, but rather to be dependent upon the personalities of the actors involved. Thus, some women will simply and openly ask, confident that if it is in their brother's power, he will give or perform.

Others will make more of a project of it, pleading, joking, and touching.

> I don't ask him immediately. I go to his house first, be always cheerful, talk to them — many pretenses. When I know he is in a good mood, I ask him. For instance, they have chinaware that I love and I would like to have it. I will not ask directly. I say, "Mano, I like this chinaware." He says, "All right. If you like it, you can have it."

Sisters pay lip service to the need not to insist or in any way force a favor from their elders (though they may force younger brothers). However, depending on their need for the object or the service and their personal relation with the brother, they can bring to bear many persuasive techniques. Such techniques, of course, again change the nature of the action from succorance to dominance. Crying as a forcing technique is given up when a girl is in her teens. Some girls or women, through necessity or temperament, will ask for many more things and services than will others. The continuously supplicant learn to make jokes of their need and their perseverance.

> I request and oil. If I am asking pig food, I make a joke, "Will you please give us food? We don't have food. In fact, it's pig food I ask." Then he will be laughing and he will give.

SISTER-TO-BROTHER NURTURANCE

As children, siblings of opposite sex help each other with many tasks, particularly those more easily performed by combining their strength. They may take a bamboo pole, hang a water container from it, and each hoist one end of the pole to a shoulder. Or together they might sweep the yard. Later on, a sister might pack a lunch of cold rice in banana leaves for her brother when he goes to the sea for a day to fish or dive. She also nurtures him by giving him money and supplies when he is in need and by nursing him in times of illness. Perhaps her period of greatest nurturant activity is when he is courting and approaching marriage. When his children are baptized, she helps to secure sponsors, raise money, and assists in the kitchen. If she is the oldest sister, she will follow the much-honored custom of taking the place of the mother in anticipating and meeting his needs.

When they are growing up, a sister performs the same services for her brother that his wife will do later on — ironing for him so that he may make a good appearance in town, seeing to it that he gets his meals, and directing him in his work activities.

When an older brother is observed sitting quiet, troubled, and brooding, the sister will solicitously ask what is wrong. Depending on the trouble, she will tease or flatter him, urge him to rest, or seek a treat for him to eat. He might be troubled about losing at gambling, a rival in courtship, or gossip. She consoles him with sympathetic small talk and admonitions to dismiss the trouble from his mind.

Oddly enough, out of eight cases, a sister does not nurture in this way when it is a younger brother who is brooding or sulking. She inquires as to the cause of the trouble. He generally cites a quarrel or his inability to obtain something he wants, and in six of the eight cases studied, she backs up the punishers or deprivers rather than her brother.

Considerable contrast may be noted in the nurturance patterns to younger sisters. Although the data on relationships between sisters were scarce, what evidence there was showed high nurturance between sisters. With the younger brother, as we have shown, nurturance is minimal. Some quotations documenting this pattern follow:

I ask him what he is unhappy about. Then he would say, "Mano Doming whipped me because I did not do an errand for him"; then I would say, "It serves you right because you are lazy to do things."

I would say, "Why, what is the matter? What happened? Anything wrong?" He would tell me he had a quarrel with someone. I would scold him, saying, "Ah, it serves you right because you are always out with them." Then he would not say anything.

I ask him what is the matter. For instance, he had a quarrel with his mother-in-law because she had been gossiping. Then I say to him, "You should not talk back because she is already your parent and it is improper for a son to fight or quarrel with parents." But he would not say anything.

SISTER-TO-BROTHER OBEDIENCE

A younger brother's attempt at command may be met with amazement. "I would say to him, 'How dare you command me, I'm not your servant.'" Other sisters may obey. Some will show resentment toward such form of communication but fulfill the boy's desire. Although an insufficient number of cases preclude any statement concerning what is most typical, some idea of those factors that contribute to variance in practice is possible. A sister may obey commands because the brother is helpless in one of several ways — weak, feeble, not knowledgeable, lacks necessary stature physically or socially, or too young for the task. She may want to act as role model and, by exhibiting the desired behavior (compliance and obedience), hope to inspire the younger boy to the same. However, she may risk exposing the family to shame if the brother is driven to ask a non-family member for the object or service he cannot obtain at home. Perhaps the most typical (and this is only an educated guess) may be:

> I would do it but I say to him, "Just tell me to do it in a soft way. Don't be commanding me because I'm not your servant." Then he would laugh and say, "All right, Mana, please do this for me."

Most, but not all, sisters envision themselves as obeying any command of their older brother, whether it be to wash clothes, go to the market, gather fruit, or look for medicine. Two atypical sisters may be considered. In one case, where obedience was not reported as the customary response, the woman had a higher socioeconomic status than her brother; in another, the woman was a truculent person who disdained and ignored her brother or quarreled with him when contact was necessary. Again, the age gap between the pair is important, with the greater likelihood of obedience if the brother is considerably older. Another variable is the degree of interdependence of brother and sister. A few individuals are not so heavily dependent on a sibling's good will, though ordinarily harmony in relationships is important.

In keeping with the latitude allowed in role playing between brother and sister which we have already noted, in many circumstances women do not submit to attempts at direction. For instance, out of sheer laziness or disinterest, they may procrastinate, refuse without petulance, or excuse themselves. "I would say, 'In a minute. I'm tired.'" Some women make distinctions concerning the importance of the task. "When it comes to important things I always do them. For less important things I have some pretenses like a stomachache or a headache."

SISTER-TO-BROTHER AGGRESSION

In childhood and adult life, joking persists in which false information makes brother perform an unnecessary act or do something foolish. A sister may tell him there is bread in the box when nothing but crumbs are left or that she has palm wine for him when she does not. Pride in or concern over one's personal appearance may be attacked:

When he goes before the mirror and stays long before it, I say, "Oh, Mano, you are already so handsome there is no need going to the mirror."

A joke of the type we would avoid in our society because we attach some stigma to the condition and think it curable, follows:

He's a little bit cross-eyed and I say, "Oh, you are again looking in another direction." He will laugh.

Disobedience in this sister-brother dyad is cause for joking, as we have already noticed in the parent-child relationship. From a sister who wearied of her brother's repeated attempts at direction:

He tells me to do something. I joke first. "Oh, I am very busy. I must go somewhere first." But in fact I am ready to do it.

Some sisters cannot, or will not, make jokes to a brother. The joking relationship may be more important in childhood when they are together more of the time and when they must compromise, adapt to each other, and sometimes join forces to defend themselves in an adult world. The joking relationship is sometimes lost when, as adults, the sister and brother do not see each other often enough to maintain familiarity. Another reason they may not joke is that the brother may be sensitive or quarrelsome.

I don't joke at him. Because even if it's only a joke he will get mad. Even this morning we had an exchange of words, a little quarrel about our land. He wants to sell our land so he can go to a doctor and I don't want that.

Only one teasing incident was reported from childhood. One girl would steal her brother's toys often enough and with such successful provocation that she made him cry. An adult brother may be teased a good deal about girl friends. Siblings of opposite sex can tease each other about personal appearances and about possible love objects. A comment about his behavior as a suitor may be a guise for a grievance of another nature:

I would tease him about his girl friend especially when there were many people present. "You behave well when you are at the house of your girl friend, but when you are home, you are like a horse." He is harsh and rough at home.

Teasing a person until he is angry is acceptable behavior, if not exactly approved. A teaser usually mollifies the anger of the person being teased.

I pretend to be mad when he has told me to do something [that makes him mad].
Question: Do you mean to make him mad?
Answer: Yes, I like to make him mad sometimes. But he will get over it because I take it back afterwards.

A sister may reprimand her brother for several types of behavior which fail to meet the cultural ideals. In childhood, she will reprimand him for playing at games or in places that contain an element of risk, such as jumping from heights or dawdling along the waterfront. Reprimands in childhood are also incurred for gambling or "stealing" coconuts from grandmother. When they are adults, the most common causes for reprimand are drinking or gambling. Sisters may also complain in a reprimanding fashion if their older brothers spend too much time away from home, carousing, courting, or visiting.

Younger brothers are scolded most often for drinking, gambling, not performing their work, or failing to listen to reprimands about these or related matters. Few sisters have the temerity to scold an older brother. They say it is improper; they fear strong verbal censure or physical violence (slapping) if they should do so. One rather aggressive woman resorts to scolding when her reprimands are not heeded, "and then there is a quarrel."

In summary, in the sister-to-brother relationship a girl is highly responsible and dominant, moderately succorant, low in nurturance, moderately obedient and aggressive. If the girl is younger than her brother she will be less dominant and aggressive, and more obedient.

DISCUSSION

In this section I will: (1) consider briefly the advantage gained by using two structured interviews to elicit data about dyadic relationships, both mother-child and woman-significant other; and (2) compare the manifestation of a behavior system in the adult with the emphasis on that system in the training of the young.

Both advantages and disadvantages arise from the use of schedules and the formal interview technique. On the one hand, their use eliminates the gathering of much extraneous, peripheral, or irrelevant information. Variation in replies due to (1) wording of the question, (2) differences in facility in a second language, (3) the order of question presentation, or (4) the degree of probing is also eliminated, and a considerable advantage is thus obtained.

First, the mother-child interview (Appendix I) was considered. Although mothers were pleased and flattered to be chosen for interviews, received us with courtesy and answered eagerly at first, the interview situation was often an uncomfortable one for them. This occurred partly because the meetings were formal instead of free; practically no explanation of the questions was permitted; if the respondent did not understand the question or failed to answer, the question was repeated as frequently as four times. Mothers found this procedure embarrassing. Furthermore, they were not trained to analytic thinking and when their answers were judged not pertinent, they were baffled by a repetition of the question.

Village mothers are not experienced in verbalizing many of the aspects of daily life which are of special interest to the investigator. Many of the customs of child rearing are taken for granted, are assumed to be perfectly natural, and are not known to be worthy of note or mention. People everywhere live by many unstated premises about the nature of human nature. A tacit understanding of the normal relations between elders and children facilitates familial relations but it makes the task of talking about those relations difficult. The use of a standard schedule and a formal interview technique in the village blocked communication some of the time. The rules for the administration of a rigidly structured schedule provided a situation highly unnatural to the Filipinos; it is less so to many Americans. Nonetheless, the use of a structured schedule is justified because of the quality of the information gathered. I obtained a great deal of material that was useful because it is focused on delimitable and important relationships. Internal consistency and checks made external to the data support confidence in the material. The material was gathered economically both in terms of time and energy.

In the mother-significant other interview (Appendix II), the same advantages and disadvantages prevailed. However, in the administration of the second interview, my assistants and I were less formal and more permissive and indulgent than we were in the first interview. It should also be noted that the mothers and I were rather well acquainted by this time, so that some of the strangeness and uneasiness (if either had been present) was diminished or not present in the second interview situation.

Some differences appeared in the quality of the material gathered in the mother-child interview versus the mother-significant other interview. In the first, the mother is talking about relatively recent events; in the second interview, the woman may either talk about recent events or she may roam farther in time to choose her answer from earlier events and experiences. In both interviews the mother is talking about herself and one other, but in the mother-child interview the other is a junior and a culture receiver. In the second interview, the woman, in at least two of the dyads and perhaps five of them, is talking about a senior and the woman herself is, perhaps more often than not, a culture receiver.

In the presentation of the material as mother-child relationships, the data were primarily abstractions and generalizations which I had made. In the presentation of the material on the mother-significant other relationships, I have used verbatim quotations liberally and also made generalizations. I hope that by so doing I have presented the reader with an intimate picture of ideals and actual behavior between individuals in certain relationships to each other. I hope, by such a presentation, to make explicit and concrete the abstractions that anthropologists make about social structure. The data presented are not, of course, all the material on which the summary descriptive statements were based, for to give the complete basis would be an impossible task. To tell all the events and happenings through which a fieldworker gains his understanding of a given system would entail a most cumbersome kind of self-consciousness and watchfulness; an anthropologist would have to go about his work with a large mirror held up to himself and to each informant. He would mentally say, "Now I am hearing such and such and in general terms it means . . ." Such a methodologically conscious anthropologist would not only have to be aware of learning each and every bit of the mosaic, but he should have to make a record of it. In other words, he should document, bit by painful bit, the accumulated knowledge on which his later summaries are based. This cannot be done. Or, at least, if it can be done, the cost in time and energy in such laborious notetaking is so great that very little actual knowledge of the subject culture will be gained and the original purpose is defeated.

A more practical solution is adopted. As much of the basis for knowledge as can be conveniently recorded is recorded. But much of what is observed (fleeting glances, a sudden rigidity or impassivity, or a flurry of activity where none seemed indicated) is interpreted and incorporated into descriptive or summary statements without actually presenting to the reader (or preserving in field notes for colleagues) the thousand and one impressions and perceptions on which the knowledge is based.

Let us turn to another area where the bases for our knowledge need continual scrutiny and appraisal.

Because of the extensive theory about connections between child-training practices and the behavior of the adult into whom that child grows, it is important at this juncture to review our findings of emphases in child training in this village and the appearance of that system of behavior in the adult. Such a review of findings may throw light on the disturbing problems with which the personality concept and related concepts are beset.[6]

In attempting to relate the patterns of childhood with the traits of adults, I find that one frequent difficulty is that the influences and the customs which shape the adult whom one studies may not be the same influences and customs as shape the children. Such a difficulty is compounded in a modern, heterogeneous population, but is minimized in a small, comparatively stable population such as is found in the village. Still, the question must be raised. How similar were the norms in which the mothers were raised to the norms in which they are raising their children? It can be confidently stated that an extensive and pervasive continuity of training occurred in the two generations involved. A third generation need not be considered because the children had to be age three to ten to be included in the study and, as a result, the mothers fell into the age range of twenty-five to forty-eight. Confidence in the continuity of training is bolstered by a number of impressions and observations about the stability of culture patterns in the rural Philippines. Naturally, some variation exists from village to village, but inquiry into specific practices in Guinhangdan indicated that many customs are unchanged or very little changed since an indeterminate time in the past. Communication with people outside the confines of the village remains very limited; considerable resistance prevails to innovations; and most of the marriages are contracted within the village.[7] All of these factors encourage continuity and stability. In addition, the very same women who were our informants on child-training practices, that is, who gave information on the way they were bringing up their children, were the respondents who informed us about their own behavior in various dyadic relationships.

First, let us examine succorance training and the expression of succorance in adult behavior. We have seen that the child is nurtured when succorant not only by the mother but also by father, siblings, and secondary and tertiary relatives. The child, then, has a wide circle of people who respond positively and rewardingly to him when he behaves succorantly. Although the experience of individuals will show some variation, it can nonetheless be said that the younger the child, the more continuous and tender the care the child will receive. The amount of reward for succorant behavior diminishes as the child grows until, at about the age of five to seven, the child is assumed to have reached a plateau of understanding, in the wake of which succorant behavior is much less appropriate and may be deliberately overlooked or punished. The degree to which succorant behavior is rewarded also varies with economic demands on the mother and other socializers. But, nevertheless, while some societies may train for a minimization of exhibition of succorance, such is not the case in the village studied (and probably in much of the Christian Philippines).

In view of the emphasis and encouragement of succorance in early childhood, do the adults show much succorance? We find that the expression of the behavior differs from dyad to dyad. A wife does not often act succorantly to a husband but does toward her father and mother. She may be freely succorant to an older sister but infrequently acts this way toward a younger one. The degree to which a woman may act succorantly to either an older sister or older brother will vary with the amount of her economic need. We are encouraged to conclude that matters other than early training in succorance are of greater importance in affecting what her action will be in a given dyadic situation. Two factors of overarching significance are economic status or need and the age of the other actor. While the sex of the other might be crucial in some societies, significantly changing the behavior when it is an intersex rather than an intrasex act, such a consideration is of minor importance in the village.

In regard to responsibility and achievement training, we have seen that the children have a substantial share in work aspects as varied as procurement and preparation of food, child care, planting or harvesting, many aspects of fishing, and in the minutiae of daily living which entail the expenditure of energy. The children are at the beck and call of any elder who needs someone to carry a message or fetch something. Drudgery is understood for what it is and the children are encouraged and coerced to assume their share. They are not trained to any personal assumption of responsibility but to await the commands and direction of others. Standards of excellence of performance were largely missing from the training of children in the village.

What about achievement in adult life? We were unable to elicit any information or to observe any evidence in behavior of the presence of such standards in the adults. Achievement as a system of behavior was not important either for the children or the adults. The villagers largely, though not entirely, lack competition as a spur to action. In areas where competition does come into play (dress, hospitality to visitors, or generosity), it is muted. Such behavior is not necessarily true among all village Filipinos. For example, Tagalogs as a group delight in open competition in the public market place.

In the husband-wife relationship, the woman carried a good deal of responsibility and had an unusual amount of decision-making power. A daughter's responsibilities to her father were more ubiquitous and binding while she was still in the parental home but continued on into her married life as well. The same is true with regard to a mother. A female has responsibilities toward both younger and older siblings but age differentials color the nature of the responsibility. A boy is especially dependent upon his sisters and other familial members when he wishes to marry.

Is the responsibility behavior system emphasized? No. Responsibility does not carry the same connotation, is not given the same weight, and does not assume the same importance as it does in our society. Work gets done eventually; the needs of the other are met in some fashion; but the whole is much more in reference to a framework of fate than it is to one's personal achievements and potential. God and nature are all-powerful. Men and women are vassals who must be subservient, respectful, submissive, and nonaggressive. In such a system, individual failures seldom need any explanation. The natural (and many of the social) causes for failure are numerous and real. Individual responsibility is minimized in a cosmos where the group and the supernatural enfold, enclose, support, protect, restrict, and loom over the individual.

"It was God's will," says the bereaved mother. "The baby was born safely, thanks to God," says the midwife. "My mother will not permit it," says a forty-year-old man, referring to an action which in our society would be autonomous, and he feels no incongruity or subservience in abiding by her decision. Responsibility is shared with fellow man and with God and other spirits. The Filipino feels at home in a pantheon; a single Deity is inconceivable. In his folklore, supernaturals occur in families, not as individuals.[8]

Responsibility and achievement are little emphasized as systems of behavior, but the same is not true of obedience. Here is an attitude and here are behaviors, the importance of which are emphasized from cradle to grave. At the beginning of one's life obedience is enforced, whereas in the later years one can exact obedience from others. But what are the norms in regard to specific dyads? In either of the daughter-parent dyads, explicit and complete submission of the child to the parent's will is expected. To one who comes from a society where such expectations do not exist, the degree to which the expectancies are met in a rural Philippine village is amazing. Children do obey their parents, in small and large matters, and for all of their lives.

Admittedly, the never-ending acts of submission to a parent and the repressing of one's will are not easily learned. As we have seen, a long period of infant indulgence is permitted before obedience training begins in earnest. During the early childhood and prepubertal years, the onus of adopting these highly submissive behaviors is alleviated somewhat by joking and procrastinating. But obedience *is* a value and individual and collective censure for disobedience are severe and pervasive. The child, the adolescent, and the young adult obey. As a young woman comes to motherhood, she, in turn, begins teaching and exacting obedience from her children.

What about the obedience relationship between siblings? The more important variable is that of age, not of sex, nor of the sibling relationship itself. Older brothers or sisters should be obeyed. The older a brother or sister is, the more imperative is the command to the younger and the fewer the reasons for not complying. Younger siblings cannot exact obedience from older ones. When we compare the amount of obedience demanded and received in the parent-child relationship as contrasted with the sibling relationship, we see that there is more flexibility in the latter dyad. There is no reason for disobeying a parent; there are several, and some of them minor in nature, for evading the wishes of a sibling.

Viewed in another way, in the parent-child dyad the positions themselves ensure responses with a high degree of predictability. But in the sibling dyad, the personal moods and recent interaction patterns of the two influence the permissible response to a greater degree. In the brother-sister dyad, the two are more dependent on their personal qualities than on their role positions for what they must do for each other.

Two more behavior systems remain to be discussed: dominance and aggression. Tendencies toward dominance and aggression in children are deplored, censured, and punished. Children of both sexes and all ages are discouraged from this behavior. And yet, when we look at the adult female, we find she is a highly dominant individual. Her dominance over her husband and her manifestations of aggressions to him are remarkable. While it is part of her role to direct the sequence of work and to control the family purse strings, this does not explain her aggression.

In the parental dyads, attempts at aggression or dominance on the part of a daughter are rare and muted. Only the indirect and less obtrusive techniques of directing another, such as flattery and bribery, are used. The daughter rationalizes such techniques as requests for the help of another rather than attempts to achieve one's will. The emphasis in the parental relationship is on contrasting systems of behavior which make directive and punitive actions inappropriate, dissonant, and incongruous. In light of a widespread usage of teasing and joking as a sanction, it is interesting to note that these two behaviors are not missing from the parent-daughter dyads but that the subjects through which they may be indulged are limited.

Although aggression is part of the sibling relationship, the amount and kind which may be displayed or indulged is more a function of age than of any other variable. Again, the older is the more aggressive and, again, aggressive impulses in a younger toward an older actor must be inhibited, even though the age difference may be negligible.

The present study has attempted a description of a Visayan agricultural-fishing village with special emphasis on the role of woman and the child-training practices. The material in this monograph should be useful in examining the hypotheses of Whiting, Lynch, Fischer, Tirykian, Eggan, and others. I submit this data for corroboration, modification, or disputation.

In this chapter we have been concerned with the role of a woman vis-à-vis significant others: husband, father, mother, sister, and brother. The role behaviors have been described in reference to systems of responsibility, dominance, succorance, nurturance, obedience, and aggression. Summaries of the role in each dyad and for each behavior system followed each subsection. The final discussion contained a note on the use of structured interviews and compared the manifestation of a behavior system in the adult with the emphasis of that system in the young.

Appendix I

SCHEDULE FOR STUDY OF MOTHER-CHILD RELATIONSHIP
1. First we want to ask you about who takes care of X. Who does
   this mostly now?
   First   want   we   ask   who   takes care   of X
   Siahan gusto namon ipakiana kon hino it nag mamangno kan X.
   Who   mostly   takes care   him   now
   Hino it ferme nga nag mamango haiya yana?
   a. How about when X was a baby?
      Who   when   small   yet he
      Hino man han gutiay pa hiya?
   b. How about your husband? Now? When X was a baby?
      How about your husband   Now   When   small   yet
      Iton imo asawa? Yana? Han hi X guti-ay pa?
2. What do you do when X asks for help or reassurance?
   What do you   when   X asks for   help   or
   Guin a-ano mo man kon hi X na-aro hin pakitabag og
      reassurance
      tambulig?
   a. How about when he falls or gets a little scratch?
      What do you   when he   falls   or   scratch
      Guin a-ano mo man kon hiya nahuhulog o napipilasan?
   b. How about when he asks you to fix something or do something?
      What do you when   asks   you   to   fix
      Guin a-ano mo kon sinusugo ka niya papag ayad hin
      something or when   ask   you   to do   something
      bisan la ano o kon sinusugo ka pa pag himo hin bisan la ano?
   c. How about when he can really do it himself?
      When   can do   really he it   himself
      Kon baga nahihimo gud niya ito hin hiya la?

   d. How about when you are busy doing something else?
      When plenty you work   and ask do you he
      Kon damo it imo trabajo nga sinusugo ka niya hin
        something
      bisan la ano?
3. Now think back when X was a baby. What do you do when he
   cried? Example: all babies cry, of course. What did you usually do
   when X cried when he was very little?
      Think   when X small yet What do you   when he
      Panumdum dao han hi X guti-ay pa. Guin a-ano mo man kon hiya
         cried   Example   Naturally   all
      nag toto-ok? Pananglitan: Natural namanla nga ngatanan it
         babies   cry   What   usually   you   do   when
      mga bata nag toto-ok. Ano man ferme an imo binubuhat kon hi
      X   cried when small yet he
      X nag toto-ok han guti-ay pa hiya.
   a. How quickly would you try to tend to him?
      Do   attend to   you him at once
      Ano man tinitimangno mo hiya dayon?
   b. How about when you were busy?
      When much you work
      Kon duro an imo trabajo?
   c. How about at night?
      At night   attend   you him at once
      Kon gab-i tinitimangno mo hiya dayon?
   d. How did other members of the household feel about his crying?
      How   feel   other   members
      Ano man it pamiti og na-onan-o man it iba nga kaorosa mo
      of household about   crying the baby's
      hin panimalay mahitungod hit pag tino-ok hit bata?
4. In your opinion do children express their feelings or keep them to
   themselves?
      In your   opinion children do express   their
      It haimo nga opinion it kabata-an nag papagawas ba hit ira
      feelings or   keep   themselves
      binabati o kon guin hihinimos la nira?
   a. Have you allowed X to express his feelings?
      you Have allowed   X to express   his feelings
      Imo naba tinugutan hi X pag pagawas hit iya binabati?
   b. How about laughing?
      When he is laughing what do you with him
      Kon hiya nag titinawa guin a-ano mo man hiya?

c. Being excited?
   When   very much is he happy what do   you
   Kon na o-ora-ora it iya kalipay guin a-ano mo man?
d. Showing anger?
   When he   shows   anger
   Kon hiya nag papakita hin kasina?
e. Crying?
   When is crying   he what do   you
   Kon nag titino-ok hiya guin a-ano mo man?

5 . When did you feel that X was old enough to start training him to
take care of himself?
   How   old was X when you   feel   old enough he
   Mag pera na an idad ni X han imo pag abat nga sadang na hiya
   start   training to   take care   himself
   tikangan pag totdo hin pag mangno haiya la ngahaw?
   a. How about feeding himself?
      How about picking food eat himself
      Iton pag pupurot pag kaon hin hiya la?
   b. How about dressing himself?
      How about dressing   himself
      Iton pag babado hin hiya la?
   c. How about playing away from the house?
      How about playing   away from   house
      Iton pag momolay gawas dida hit panimalay?
   d. Did you try to teach him to do these things or did he just learn
      by himself?
      Did try you to teach him these or did   learn   just
      Nag sari ka pag totdo haiya hini o kon nahabaro la hin
      himself
      iya la?

6. Tell me about how you taught X to fetch water to help you?
   Tell   me   how   you   taught   X fetch water
   Sumati dao ako kon inonan-o mo an pag totdo kan X pag alog?
   a. What did you do about it?
      What do you   about   it
      Nag ano kaman mahitungod hini?

7. What chores do you expect X to do? How often does he have to
   do this — is it regularly?
   What   are   works   you   expect   to   work
   Ano man nga trabajo-on it imo guin lalauman nga tatrabajo-on
      X   Does he   work this   regularly
   ni X? Ano it iya pag trabajo hini — sukot ba?

    a. How did you get him to do them?

       How did   you   get   do   him them

       Inonan-o man nimo nga mag trabajo hiya hito?

    b. What happens if X fails to do them?

       What if   X does not the   do   work

       Ano ma kon hi X dire hito nga sugo nag tatrabajo?

8. Do you expect X to obey immediately when you ask him to do something or do you give him a little leeway? Are you patient?

   Do expect you   X obey   immediately you ask do

   Nag lalaum kaman nga hi X masugot dayon kon imo sinusugo hin

   something or do you   give   little   leeway

   bisan la ano o kon imo anay tinatagan hin gutiay nga ligoy?

   patient   you Are

   Pacencioso kaba?

    a. What if he dawdles or delays?

       What   if   dawdles   he or   delays

       Ano man kon nahamamalanga hiya o nalilibang?

    b. Do you always do this or do you sometimes let it go?

       always You this   do   or do sometimes let it

       Ferme mo ini guin bubuhat o kon danay mo la ini

       go

       pabaya-an?

9. How satisfied do you feel when X does things well? Give examples.

   How   are   you   contented much or little just if   X

   Ma-onan-o man it imo ka kontento, duro o guti-ay la kon hi X

       works   well   Give

   nag tratrabajo hin maopay? Tagui dao hin pananglitan o

   examples

   ejemplo

    a. What do you do when he does something well?

       What do   you he   when   works   well

       Ina-ano-an man nim hiya kon nag tratrabajo hin maopay?

    b. Do you care more about his getting them done or doing them especially well?

       care you Do that   his work   done   just or   want

       Karoyag mo ba nga it iya trabajo mahuman la o kon karoyag

       you do the best   done work

       mo gud it puerte gud nga ka trabajo?

    c. What do you do if he is careless?

       What do   you   when poor   is his work

       Guin a-ano mo man kon dire asya it iya trabajo?

10. How do you feel about having friends for your children?

    How do   you feel   or think   about   friends   for

Ano man it imo pamati o huna-huna tungod hit kasankayan hit
your children
imo mga anak?

a. Do you wish that X would play alone more or with the group
more?
   wish you Do that more   X would play   alone or do
   Karoyag mo ba nga kaorog hi X mag molay hit iya la o kon
   want you   more   him play   with   the group
   karoyag mo nga kaurog it iya molay mahatampo hin gropo?

b. What do you do about it?
   What   do you   do   about   it
   Ano man it imo binubuhat mahitungod hini?

c. Is there any one you'd rather your child didn't play with? Why?
   Anyone you'd rather have him play with? Why?
   Is there   child   don't you   want   to   play with your
   May ada ba bata nga dire mo karoyag nga igkamolay hit imo
   child   Who   and   why   Is there   child
   anak? it hin-o ngan kay ano? May ada liwat bata nga
   want   you   only   him to play with   Who   and   why
   karoyag mo sayla niya igkamolay? It hin-o ngan kay ano?

11. Do you think X should help younger children when they are in
difficulty or do you think he should mind his own business?
Do you   think   should   X   help   those
Haimo nga hunahuna kinahanglan ba nga hi X mabulig hadton
children   younger   who   need   help
kabata-an nga maromanghod niya nga naninginahanglan hin bulig,
or if   leave   he'll   and   mind just   his   own
o kon pababaya-an niya ngan mag tikos la hit iya la nga osa?

a. Could you give an example of what you've done when this
came up?
   Could give you   an   example   of   what you've   done
   Maka hatag ka ba hin pananlitan kon nag ano ka o guin ano
   when   came this up   time
   mo han pag abot hini nga higayon?

12. Do you like to see children take up leadership? Do you feel this
makes them bossy?
   like   Do you   see   when   children   take up   they
   Naroroyag ka ba pagkita kon iton kabata-an ginagamit nira it
            leadership   feel Do you   think
   pag paka leader-leader? Pamati mo it haim nga huna huna hi
     make   them   bossy
   dadaras-an ba nira it pag paka mayor-mayor?

a. What do you do about this with X?

What   do you   with   X   about   this

Guin a-ano mo man hi X mahitungod hini?

13. What do you do when X tries to get his own way with you?

What   do you   do   when   X tries   to get   his

Ano man it imo binubuhat kon hi X nag papaturon la hit hiya

own   way with you

karoyag sidngon haimo?

a. How about when he does this with other children?

When he this   does   with other   children   what do

Kon iya ini guin bubuhat hit iba nga kabata-an guin a-ano

you

mo man?

14. How about when X is playing with one of the other children in the neighborhood and there is a quarrel or fight — how do you handle this?

How about when X   is   playing   with one of children   in

Ano man kon hi X nakikig molay hin osa nga bata dida hit

neighborhood and there is   quarrel or fight

pag higrani nga nag kaka ada in away o sontokay? —

How do   you   handle   this

ino-onan-o mo man it pag tuhay hini?

a. Do you ever feel that X is too touchy?

feel Do you touchy   X

Pamati mo madulo ba hi X?

b. Do you ever encourage X to fight back?

you Do   X   ever   encourage   fight back

Imo ba hi X guin a-aghat pag pa bulos o pag pa ato?

15. Sometimes children are angry at their parents when they are being criticized or scolded. How do you handle this with X?

Sometimes children   angry at their   parents when   scolded

Osahay it kabata-an nasisina hit ira kag-anak kon guin bubusa-an

or when criticized What do you   with X about   this

o kon sinususnan. Guin a-ano mo man hi X mabitungud hini?

a. Could you give an example of this?

Could give you   an   example   this

Maka hatag ka ba hin pananglitan hini?

b. What if he kicks you or strikes you?

What   if   kick   you he or   strike you

Ano man kon banyakan ka niya o kon ato han ka?

16. Some parents have trouble keeping their child from being mean to smaller children and bullying them Have you managed this?

Some   parents have trouble   in   managing their

May ada mga kaganak nga kinukurian hit pag suhito hit ira mga
child   fond of bullying   smaller than they
anak nga mag lupig o maraog daog hit gurogudti haira nga
children   you Have managed   this
kabata-an. Ikao naka suhito ka ba hini?
children   you Have managed   this
a. How about teasing?
   How about teasing
   Iton kama sunglog?

17. Could you tell me who in the household has the main charge of X
to see that he behaves? Who usually disciplines X when he is
naughty? When several are present?
   Could   tell   you   who   in   your household has
   Makakag sumat ka ba kon hin-o dinhe hit iyo panimalay it nag
   charge   of X   behaves   Who usually
   mamangno gud kan X nga dire mapapag sinaway? Hin-o ferme it
   disciplines   X when   naughty Who   when several
   nadisciplina kan X kon nag pipinilyo? Hin-o man kon damo it
   present   here
   presente o kon damo dinhe haiyo?
   a. (If husband) Do you ever? (if wife) Does your husband ever?
      If   husband Do discipline you ever if   wife   Does
      (Kon it asawa) Na disciplina ka ba? (kon it asawa) It
      your husband   discipline ever
      imo asawa na disciplina ba?
   b. How about X's older sibling (if he has one)
      Does X's older sibling   discipline   too   if   has   he
      It kan X kamagurangan na suhito guihapon? (kon may ada niya)
   c. How about others in the household? (nurse, baby sitters, grand-
      parents, uncles, aunts, etc.)
      Do others in   household   discipline   too
      Iton iba dinhi hit iyo panimalay nag susuhito guihapon?
      nurse, baby sitter, grandparents, aunts,   uncles   etc.
      (nars, paralibang, ka-apoyan, kadada-an, kabata-an iba pa.)

18. If Y (the person who usually punishes X) is not there who usually
takes over?
   If   Y   who usually   punishes   not there who
   Kon hi Y (iton ferme nga parahatag hin sirot) waray dida hin-o
         takes over
   man it na saliwan?
   a. Is Y mentioned when someone else punishes X?
      Is Y   mentioned   when others   punishes

Hi Y hin ngangaranan man niya kon iba it nagkakastigo
X
haiya?

19. When X is naughty how is he usually punished?
When X is   naughty how is   usually   punished he
Kon hi X nag pipinilyo ano man it ferme nga pag kastigo haiya?
  a. How about spanking?
     How about spanking used is it also   as punishment
     Iton pag lagpak guinagamit ini guihapon niyo nga kastigo?
  b. How about not letting him have something he wants?
     How about not giving him   wants   punishment also
     Iton dire pag tatagui hit iya kinaroroyag kastigo guihapon
     is it
       ini niyo?
  c. How about making fun of him?
     How about making fun used is it   also   as punishment
     Iton pag sunglog ginagamit ini guihapon nga kastigo niyo?
  d. How about not speaking to him?
     How about not   speaking   him   used   also   is it
     Iton dire pakikihimangrawi haiya ginagamit guihapon ini
     punishment
     nga kastigo?
  e. How about sending him to another room?
     How about sending him   to room
     Iton pag papakadto-a hiya ha sulod?
  f. How about warning him about the bogey man?
     How about warning about bogey man
     Iton pag tatarhuga hit aswang?
  g. How about threatening to send him away?
     How about threatening send away him
     Iton pag tatarhuga pag paiwasa haiya?
  h. How about referring to God?
     How about referring to God
     Iton pag tatarhuga han diyos?
  i. How about kneeling?
     How about kneeling
     Iton pag papaludha?
  j. How about pinching?
     How about pinching
     Iton pag kukuribota?

20. What methods do you use (if she disciplines) most frequently?
    What   methods of punishment (if   she   disciplines)
    Ano nga pa-agui hin kastigo (kon hiya it na disciplina)

do you frequently   use
it imo masukot gamiton?
a. How about your husband (if he disciplines)?
How about husband (if   he   disciplines)
Iton imo asawa   (kon hiya it na disciplina)?
b. How about others in the household (if they discipline)?
How about others   in   household (if   they
Iton iba nga kaorosa niyo hin panimalay (kon hira it na
discipline)
disciplina)?

21. Do you do anything special when X is good?
Is there you anything do   special   X when   is
May ada mo nahihimo nga special para kan X kon hiya nag
good
mamaopay?
a. What about special gifts?
How about special   gifts do give you
Iton special nga regalo or suhol na hatab ka?
b. Privileges?
How about special privileges do give   you   also
Iton special nga priviligio na hatag ka guihapon?
c. Allowances?
How about money allowances give you
Iton kuarta nga suhol na hatag ka?
d. Praise?
Do praise you
Na dayao ka haiya?
e. Kissing?
About kissing,   kiss   you do
Pag harok, na harok ka?
f. Stroking?
About stroking
Pag hapohap?

Appendix II

SCHEDULE FOR STUDY OF DYADIC RELATIONSHIPS OF WOMEN

1. What are the duties of a (wife, daughter, sister, etc.) toward an X? What else?
   a. Are you able to fulfill these obligations most of the time? Example?
   b. Are there some times when you do not? Example?
2. What do you do when you are trying to get X to do some work for you or to do you a favor? Example? Then what? Do you oil? Kneel? Caress?
   a. What if he doesn't want to do it? Did you ever force?
   b. Do you get X to do it most of the time or do you give in most of most of the time? Why?
3. When you wish X would give you something, what do you do? Example? Oil? Kneel? Caress?
   a. What if he doesn't want to give it?
   b. Does X give it to you most of the time or do you give up most of the time? Why?
4. Do you help X when he is in need? Could you give us an example of that?
   a. How about when he is feeling said or unhappy? What do you do? Example? Oil? Kneel? Caress?
   b. Do you feel that you like to take care of X? In what ways? Why?
5. What do you do if X commands you to do something? Example?
   a. What if you don't want to do it?
   b. Do you obey most of the time or do you refuse most of the time? Why?
6. What are some of the things you joke X about?
   a. What are some of the things you tease X about?
   b. Can you give us an example of a time when you reprimanded him? Another?
   c. What are some of the things you scold X about?

Notes

PREFACE

1. The field work was made possible by a Fulbright grant, which was later extended. For this basic bounty I am grateful, but my gratitude is for far more than the necessary monetary support. The administrative personnel of the Fulbright Foundation in the Philippines were unfailingly encouraging and helpful before, during, and after the year of research. My special thanks are due Dr. Alfred Morales, Jose Orozco of the United States Educational Foundation, Dr. H. Otley Beyer of the Museum of Archaeology and Ethnology, and to numerous friends on the faculties of the University of the Philippines and Silliman University. The World Health Organization had a research center for the study of schistosomiasis near Palo, Leyte. I am indebted to them for much help, but in particular to Drs. T. P. Pesigan, Farooq, Nelson Hairston, and Mr. and Mrs. Juaregi.

2. John M. Whiting *et al., Field Guide for a Study of Socialization in Five Societies,* mimeographed (Cambridge: Laboratory of Human velopment, Harvard University, 1953).

3. B. B. Whiting, ed., *Six Cultures: Studies of Child Rearing* (Cambridge: Laboratory of Human Development, Harvard University, 1963).

2: THE SETTING

1. Officially the location of the Islands as a whole is cited as 21°20' north and 4°30' north latitude and 116°55' east and 126° east latitude. *Statistical Handbook of the Philippines 1903–1953* (Manila: Bureau of the Census and Statistics, Department of Commerce and Industry, 1954).

2. G. B. Cressey, *Asia's Lands and People* (New York: McGraw-Hill Book Co., 1944).

3. *Ibid.*

4. The reconstruction given in the following account is based on interviews with two of the oldest, most verbal, and most historical-minded men in the village; on interviews with younger but better-educated men and women; on a typewritten report prepared by the principals, head teachers, and class teachers (Historical Data and Cultural Life of the People of Palo, Leyte, and Her Barrios [1953, on file at Palo Library, Leyte]); and on talks with priests who resided in the neighborhood.

5. The Tagalogs are still differentiated from the main population. On the one hand, they have retained their own dialect although they also speak Waray Waray. On the other hand, there have been five cases of intermarriage with Guinhangdan people.

6. John H. Romani, "The Philippine Barrio," *Journal of Asian Studies*, 15:2 (February, 1956), 229.

7. Generosa F. Rivera and Robert T. McMillan, *The Rural Philippines* (Manila: Office of Information Mutual Security Agency, 1952).

8. Romani, *op. cit.*, 230.

9. *Ibid.*, 234.

10. Willis E. Sibley, "Leadership in a Philippine Barrio," *Philippine Journal of Public Administration*, 1 (April, 1957), 155.

3: SOCIOECONOMIC STRUCTURE

1. Melville Herskovits, *Economic Anthropology* (New York: Alfred A. Knopf, 1953), pp. 88–91.

2. Charles J. Erasmus, "Work Patterns in a Mayo Village," *American Anthropologist*, 57:2 (1955), 322–33.

3. For proof that these difficulties with the concept "occupation" are not limited to traditional, peasant, or village societies, see Edward Gross, "The Occupational Category in Research," *American Sociological Review*, 24:5 (October, 1959), 640–49. Gross discusses the concept in connection with the United States Census. He points out the need for special attention to part-time jobs and multiple job holdings as part of the variable, "occupation."

4. *Census of the Philippines, 1948* (Manila: Bureau of the Census and Statistics, Department of Commerce and Industry).

5. See also Oscar Lewis, *Life in a Mexican Village: Tepoztlan Restudied* (Urbana: University of Illinois Press, 1951), pp. 118 ff. In eight barrios in Tepoztlan, Mexico, Lewis found that the land-owning families were, respectively, 26 per cent, 26 per cent, 27 per cent, 33 per cent, 38 per cent, 41 per cent, 53 per cent, and 61 per cent of the whole. The size of these barrios ranges from 22 to 223 family units. The last is nearest the size of Guinhangdan and their percentages may be compared. The Mexican village had 27 per cent and Guinhangdan 42 per

cent who were landowners. Startling as the Guinhangdan figures are, they do not represent the worst case of landless people.

Lewis also found that the distribution of land ownership in itself was not an accurate index to barrio wealth, for some villages which had a high percentage of landowners were wealthy villages and some were not. I found this to be true of individuals as well as of villages. The fact of ownership and the amount of land did not automatically make a family wealthy. For one thing, not all land is cultivated. For another, not all land is equally good. Yet, despite this, land acquisition and ownership are important goals to the inhabitants of Guinhangdan and the size of a family's holdings is of interest to all.

Lewis' findings about the size of holdings are similar. Out of 853 family units in eight barrios, only 3.3 per cent had holdings of more than fifteen hectares. The two largest holdings were twenty-five and twenty-nine hectares. The percentage of owners with less than a hectare was 36.2 per cent or three and one-half times as large as that of Guinhangdan. In this and the previous comparison, Lewis' figures refer to privately held lands only.

6. Leonard Broom and Philip Selznick, *Sociology* (Evanston, Ill.: Row, Peterson and Company, 1955), pp. 167–87.

7. Education is another criterion that is frequently used. In fact, education, occupation, and income are the triad on which many a stratification study in America is raised. Education was not applicable as an indicator of social class in the village, or, more accurately, was only partially applicable. Although the reasons are several, probably the most important is that education does not guarantee increased money income nor provide the channel for upward mobility that it does in America. This, in turn, is based on the underdeveloped state of economy, the under- and unemployment, and the lack of capital and entrepreneurs. A separate reason is that the quality of education leaves much to be desired.

8. Frank Lynch, *Social Class in a Bikol Town* (Chicago: The University of Chicago Press, 1959), pp. 89–91. The emphasis of the study is on methodology.

9. *Ibid.*, pp. 115–17.

10. Edward A. Tirykian, "The Prestige Evaluation of Occupations," *American Journal of Sociology*, 63 (January, 1958), 390–400.

4: HOUSEHOLD COMPOSITION

1. See Chapter 3, "Socioeconomic Data: Source Material."

2. This type is called dependent nuclear by G. P. Murdock, *Social Structure* (New York: Macmillan Co., 1949), p. 22.

144   Notes

3. J. L. Fischer, "The Classification of Residence in Censuses," *American Anthropologist*, 60 (June, 1958), 508–17.

4. W. H. Goodenough, "Residence Rules," *Southwestern Journal of Anthropology*, 12 (Spring, 1956), 22–37.

5. *Ibid.*, par. 4.

6. Paul Bohannan, "An Alternate Residence Classification," *American Anthropologist*, 59 (February, 1957), 126–39.

7. Murdock, *op. cit.*, 2.

8. Meyer Fortes, *Web of Kinship* (London: Oxford Univ. Press, 1949). Cited in Jack Goody, "The Fission of Domestic Groups among the Lodagaba," in *The Developmental Cycle in Domestic Groups, Cambridge Papers in Social Anthropology*, No. 1 (New York, 1958), p. 53.

9. Meyer Fortes, "Introduction to the Developmental Cycle in Domestic Groups," *op. cit.*, 1–14.

10. Fred Eggan, *Social Organization of the Western Pueblos* (Chicago: University of Chicago Press, 1950), p. 9; Murdock, *op. cit.* (1949), 1; Fischer, *op. cit.* (1958), 508; and M. J. Levy, Jr., and L. A. Fallers, "The Family: Some Comparative Considerations," *American Anthropologist*, 61 (August, 1959), 650.

11. Fallers, *op. cit.*, 650.

5: Mother and Child in Guinhangdan

1. G. P. Murdock, *op. cit.* Pp. 94 ff. contains the definitions here used.

2. Several people have been most helpful to me in formulating the introduction to this chapter and in the terminology section. I have drawn freely from Alfred Evangelista, *The Nipa Community of Bubog Paombong, Bulacan, Philippines* (unpublished master's thesis, University of Chicago, 1959), from letters and the published works of Frank Lynch, and from the considerate help of Lee Guemple and Maria Redona. Evangelista has a fine section on an individual's perception of his kin and the conditions which limit such perception. See pp. 24 ff.

3. Frank Lynch, *Social Class in a Bikol Town* (Chicago: University of Chicago Press, 1959), p. 24.

4. Ethel Nurge, "Cultural Factors Operative in Mate Selection in a Philippine Village," *Eugenics Quarterly*, 5:3 (1958), 162–68. When I wrote this article, I thought residence was not patterned. Additional analysis of material untouched to that time revealed a pattern.

5. F. Lynch, personal communication to the author.

6. A. L. Kroeber, "Classificatory Systems of Relationship," *Journal of the Royal Anthropological Institute*, 39 (January–June, 1909), 77–84.

7. Agaton P. Pal, "A Philippine Barrio: Social Organizations in Relation to Planned Cultural Change," *University of Manila Journal of East Asiatic Studies*, 4 (October, 1956), 333–486.

8. *Ibid.*, 337.

9. *Ibid.*, 382.

10. *Ibid.*, 383.

11. *Ibid.*, 391.

12. D. M. Schneider and G. C. Homans, "Kinship Terminology and the American Kinship System," *American Anthropologist*, 57 (December, 1955), 1194–207. See pp. 1195 ff.

13. *Ibid.*, 1203.

14. The definitions of the behavior systems have been adopted with modifications. My debt to Whiting and his associates is considerable.

15. An exception must be noted. A mother who had lived away from the village for a short period and who prides herself on her modernity boasted that her child could pick food from the plate at eight months.

16. Soft words, interestingly enough, are an ideal form of behavior for many occasions other than dyadic relationships between caretaker and child. For instance, in bargaining for an item of purchase or an advantage of some sort, one begins in a soft, deprecating voice which becomes a stylized whine. Also, when in the presence of sorcerers, witches, or spirits, one should speak softly in order not to startle or anger them. To rid a field of rats, one must walk softly, talk softly, and show no anger.

17. See Ethel Nurge, "Economic Functions of the Child in the Rural Philippines," *Philippine Sociological Review*, 4 (January, 1956), 7–11, for comparative material on children in another village.

18. The role model which the socializer deems suitable for the child is connected with the self-image of a given individual, so that a mother who is a teacher and feels herself a leader in that role likes to see similar behavior in her little girl's play.

19. Sometimes the child runs away for a short period of time to another household. He may go for an extended visit to a loving and indulgent kin. The parents then have time to "cool off." I have no frequency counts on this visiting pattern but it seems to be fairly common.

20. Bartlett H. Stoodley, "Some Aspects of Tagalog Family Structure," *American Anthropologist*, 59 (April, 1957), 236–49. The present quotation is from page 241.

21. Ethel Nurge, "Economic Functions of the Child in the Rural Philippines," *op. cit.*, 7–11.

22. David C. McClelland and G. A. Friedman, "A Cross-Cultural Study of the Relationship Between Child Training Practices and Achievement Motivation Appearing in Folktales," in *Readings in Social Psychology*, Theodore M. Newcomb and Eugene L. Hartley, eds. (New York: Henry Holt and Co., 1952), pp. 247 ff.

23. George M. Guthrie. The data came from "Social Class and Na-

tional Differences in Child Bearing Attitudes," *The Filipino Child and Philippine Society* (Manila: Philippine Normal College Press, 1961).

6: DYADIC RELATIONSHIPS IN THE FAMILY

1. Whiting, *op. cit.*
2. For a discussion of some problems in interviewing, see chap. 5, "Mother to Child Relationships: Source Material." Dyadic relationship interviews were considerably less formal than mother-child interviews.
3. Oliver Douglas, "An Ethnographer's Method for Formulating Descriptions of 'Social Structure,'" *American Anthropologist*, 60 (October, 1958), 801–26.
4. In the context of child care interviews, six mothers were asked about the division of decision making. Four mothers say that they make most of the decisions about the children; two say both the father and the mother. Four mothers decide how far from home the child may wander; in two families, both the father and the mother make the decision. In matters of health, such as whether or not to keep a child indoors for a day or to send for the curer, the mothers again are the major agents. In the matter of initiation into economic role, both the age and sex of the child are relevant. For children six to ten, the mother is the main task-giver regardless of the sex of the child. If the decision is whether or not to move to a different house, in three instances it is made by the husband, in two by both, and in one case by the wife. It should be recognized that the division on decision making might be reported differently if the fathers were interviewed. They were not interviewed about these specific questions but their accounts of dyadic relationships with women (see material that follows in text) substantiates my conclusions about their minor role in decision making.
5. Ethel Nurge, "Etiology of Illness in Guinhangdan," *American Anthropologist*, 60 (December, 1958), 1158–72.
6. The culture and personality field has burgeoned. Adherence to any particular body of concepts or theory is largely a matter of group membership. All of the theories offer some insights and some promise. The techniques of data collection and analysis are useful according to the nature of the problem one is interested in or inadequate on the same criterion. The number of times that an individual investigator uses exclusively or almost wholly any one theory can often be traced to the fact that he or she is a member of a coterie or is a disciple. The generalist, the synthesizer, is not missing but that we have as yet failed to produce the good, the meaningful, the fruitful synthesis is amply testified by the fact that our work in personality and culture has had so little impact on the sister and other disciplines.

For an excellent survey of the literature, see Milton Singer's "A Survey of Culture and Personality Theory and Research," in *Studying Personality Cross-Culturally*, Bert Kaplan, ed. (Evanston, Ill.: Row, Peterson and Company, 1961). For the most recent survey, covering the literature between the "middle of 1960 and July, 1962," see Robert A. LeVine's "Culture and Personality," in *Biennial Review of Anthropology 1963*, B. J. Siegel, ed. (Stanford, Calif.: Stanford University Press, 1963).

7. Nurge, *op. cit.*, 1958.

8. Ethel Nurge, "The Nature of the Supernatural in Four Myths from Guinhangdan, Leyte, Philippines," *The Silliman Journal*, 8 (Second Quarter, 1961). Dumaguete, R.P.I. See also Francis L. K. Hsu, "Kinship and Ways of Life: An Exploration," in Hsu, ed., *Psychological Anthropology* (Homewood, Ill.: Dorsey Press, 1961).

Bibliography

[AUTHOR UNKNOWN]

1953 *Historical Data and Cultural Life of the People of Palo, Leyte, and Her Barrios.* Manuscript at Palo Library, Leyte.

BOHANNAN, PAUL

1957 "An Alternate Residence Classification," *American Anthropologist,* 59:126–39.

BROOM, LEONARD, AND PHILIP SELZNICK

1955 *Sociology.* Row, Peterson and Company, Evanston, Illinois.

BUREAU OF THE CENSUS AND STATISTICS

1954 *Statistical Handbook of the Philippines 1903–1953.* Bureau of the Census and Statistics, Philippines.

CRESSEY, G. B.

1944 *Asia's Lands and People.* McGraw-Hill Book Co., New York.

DOUGLAS, OLIVER

1958 "An Ethnographer's Method for Formulating Descriptions of Social Structure," *American Anthropologist,* 60:801–26.

EGGAN, FRED

1950 *Social Organization of the Western Pueblos.* University of Chicago Press, Chicago, Illinois.

EGGAN, FRED, et al.

1956 *Area Handbook on the Philippines.* University of Chicago for the Human Relations Area Files.

ERASMUS, CHARLES J.

1955 "Work Patterns in a Maya Village," *American Anthropologist,* 57:322–33.

EVANGELISTA, ALFRED

1959 "The Nipa Community of Bubog Paombong, Bulacan, Philippines," Unpublished master's thesis, University of Chicago, Chicago, Illinois.

FISCHER, JOHN L.

1958 "The Classification of Residence in Censuses," *American Anthropologist,* 60:508–17.

FORTES, MEYER
1949   *Web of Kinship*. London.
1958   "Introduction to the Developmental Cycle in Domestic Groups," *Cambridge Papers in Social Anthropology*, No. 1, New York.
GOODENOUGH, WARD H.
1956   "Residence Rules," *Southwestern Journal of Anthropology*, 12:22–37.
GROSS, EDWARD
1959   "The Occupational Category in Research," *American Sociological Review*, 24:640–49.
GUTHRIE, GEORGE M.
1961   *The Filipino Child and Philippine Society*. Philippine Normal College Press, Manila.
HERSKOVITS, MELVILLE
1953   *Economic Anthropology*. Alfred A. Knopf, New York.
HSU, FRANCIS L. K.
1961   "Kinship and Ways of Life: An Exploration," in *Psychological Anthropology*, ed. Francis L. K. Hsu, Dorsey Press, Homewood, Illinois.
KROEBER, A. L.
1909   "Classificatory System of Relationship," *Journal of the Royal Anthropological Institute*, 39.
LEVINE, ROBERT A.
1963   "Culture and Personality," pp. 107–45, in *Biennial Review of Anthropology 1963*, ed. B. J. Siegel, Stanford University Press, Stanford, California.
LEVY, M. J., JR., AND L. A. FALLERS
1959   "The Family: Some Comparative Considerations," *American Anthropologist*, 61:647–51.
LEWIS, OSCAR
1951   *Life in a Mexican Village: Tepoztlan Restudied*. University of Illinois Press, Urbana, Illinois.
LYNCH, FRANK
1959   *Social Class in a Bikol Town*. Research Series, No. 1, Philippine Studies Program, University of Chicago, Chicago, Illinois.
MCCLELLAND, DAVID C., AND G. A. FRIEDMAN
1952   "A Cross-cultural Study of the Relationship Between Child Training Practices and Achievement Motivation Appearing in Folktales," in *Readings in Social Psychology*, eds. Theodore M. Newcomb and Eugene L. Hartley, Henry Holt and Co., New York.

MURDOCK, GEORGE P.
   1949   *Social Structure.* Macmillan Co., New York.
NURGE, ETHEL
   1956   "Economic Functions of the Child in the Rural Philippines,"
           Philippine Sociological Review, 4:7–11.
   1958   "Cultural Factors Operative in Mate Selection in a Philippine
           Village," *Eugenics Quarterly,* 5:162–68.
   1958   "Etiology of Illness in Guinhangdan," *American Anthropologist,* 60:1158–72.
   1961   "The Nature of the Supernatural in Four Myths from Guin-
           hangdan, Leyte, Philippines," *The Silliman Journal,* Vol. 8,
           No. 2, Second Quarter, Dumaguete, R.P.I.
PAL, AGATON P.
   1956   "A Philippine Barrio: Social Organizations in Relation to
           Planned Cultural Change," *University of Manila Journal of
           East Asiatic Studies,* 4:333–486, Manila.
RIVERA, GENEROSA F., AND ROBERT T. MCMILLAN
   1952   *The Rural Philippines.* Office of Information Mutual Security
           Agency, Manila.
ROMANI, JOHN H.
   1956   "The Philippine Barrio," *Journal of Asian Studies,* 15:229–37.
SCHNEIDER, D. M., AND G. C. HOMANS
   1955   "Kinship Terminology and the American Kinship System,"
           American Anthropologist, 57:1194–207.
SIBLEY, WILLIS E.
   1957   "Leadership in a Philippine Barrio," *Philippine Journal of
           Public Administration,* 1, Manila.
SINGER, MILTON
   1961   "A Survey of Culture and Personality Theory and Research,"
           pp. 9–90, in *Studying Personality Cross-Culturally,* ed. Bert
           Kaplan, Row, Peterson and Co., Evanston, Illinois.
STOODLEY, BARTLETT H.
   1957   "Some Aspects of Tagalog Family Structure," *American An-
           thropologist,* 59:236–49.
TIRYKIAN, EDWARD A.
   1958   "The Prestige Evaluation of Occupations," *The American
           Journal of Sociology,* 63:390–400.
WHITING, BEATRICE B. (ED.)
   1963   *Six Cultures: Studies of Child Rearing.* John Wiley and Sons,
           Inc., New York.
WHITING, JOHN W. M., *et al.*
   1953   *Field Guide for a Study of Socialization in Five Societies.*
           Laboratory of Human Development, Harvard University,
           Cambridge, Mass. (Mimeo.).

Index

Abaca cloth: used in clothing, 18–19; used in footwear, 20

Abaca trees: in cultivation, 31; in ropemaking, 34

Achievement: defined, 73, 89; mother to child, 74–76, 89; compared, 82; in relation to independence training, 83; in dyadic relationships, 89; in training and adult behavior, 125–27

Age: frequency distribution of parents, 50–51; a factor in households, 50–52, 56–57, 58, 59, *passim;* comparative, spouses', 51; frequency distribution of children's, 52; categories of, 68–69; in measuring achievement, 74; in measuring responsibility, 75; factor in child training, 76–77; in play groups, 77; factor in aggression, 128

Aggression: defined, 78, 90; mother to child, 78–79, 89; compared, 82, 84; wife to husband, 95–97; daughter to father, 100; daughter to mother, 104–06; sister to sister, 111–13; sister to brother, 119–21; training and adult behavior, 128; in siblings, 128; mentioned, 110

Agriculture: as economic activity, 26; kinds of, 31; mentioned, 3. *See also* Farming

Australia, 9

Bakia, described, 20. *See also* Footwear

Bamboo: in housing, 21, 40; *photograph,* ff. 23; mentioned, 93, 114

Banana trees: in cultivation, 31

Banguio (Luzon), 9

Baptism, responsibility: of sponsor, 67; of daughter, 98; of sister, 107; of children, 117; mentioned, 67

Barrio: defined, 12, 15–16; governmental structure of, 15–18

Bohannan, Paul: on classification of residences, 60

Borneo, 9

Bukidnon (Mindanao), 9

Bunga (Leyte), 12

Camotes: in cultivation, 31; mentioned, 14, 93

Carabao: use of, in tenant farming, 32

Carigara, 13

Caroline Islands, 9

Carpenters: as occupational classification, 33, 35; relation to land ownership, 37–38; relation to cash income, 39. *See also* Occupations

Census: as tool for gathering socioeconomic data, 23, 29, 45

Childbirth, behavior patterns toward: by parents, 58; by husband, 92–93; by mother, 102; by sister, 107

Child-rearing practices: behavior patterns, 71–84; compared with American, 82–86

Children: effect of social environment, 50–63; distribution in families, 50–63; age, frequency distribution, 52; as economic factor, 53; adoptive, 55–56; age categories of, 68; relation to mother, 69–83; factors in rearing, 71–84; succorance of, 71, 72–73, 108–09, 113, 116–17; achievement, 73–76, 89; obedience, 76–77, 83–84, 89, 100, 101, 104, 106, 110, 113, 114, 118–119, 127–28; sociability of, 77–78, 84, 89; aggression, 78–79, 89; punishment of, 79–81, 84–85, 115; teasing of, 11, 80, 120; rewards, forms of, 81–82, 85; dependence, 82–84; compared with American, 82–86; dominance in, 98, 102–03, 107–08, 114–15; nurturance, 99–100, 103, 106, 109–10, 113, 117–18; training of and adult behavior, 124–29

China, 9

Clerical workers: as occupational group, 34, 35; relation to land ownership, 38; relation to cash income, 39–40; relation to social class, 43

Climate: in Philippines, 9–10

Clothing: Western influence on, 18–19; as an industry, 19; described, 18, 19–20; as criteria in defining social class, 40

Coconuts: in cultivation, 31, 32; farming of an occupation, 34; as mortgage crop, 36; mentioned, 10, 33, 93, 114, 121

Communication, problems in, 7

Cooking: facilities, 21; techniques, 91

Copra growing: as occupational classification, 26, 34; mentioned, 70

Credit. See Debt

Data: collection of, 4–5; criteria governing selection, 5–6; recording of, 6–8; kinds of, 23–24; census information as source, 23–24; sources of socioeconomic, 23–29; methods used in collecting, 24, 45–47; difficulties in establishing accuracy of, 24–25, 29; on occupations, 25–29, 33, 37–40; methods used in adjusting, 28; processing socioeconomic, 29; on land ownership, 29–31, 37–39; on land use, 31–33; on cash income, 35–37, 39–40; on social stratification, 40–44; on household composition, 45–59; on ages, 47–52. See also Interview techniques

Death, responsibility: of daughter, 98, 102; of sister, 107

Debt: significance, 36–37; relationship to creditor, 37; mentioned, 28

Dependence: in child training, 82, 83; compared, 82–84

Diet: as criteria in defining social class, 40; described, 91. See also Food

Discipline. See Punishment

Distribution of families. See Households

Divorce, rare, 53

Dominance: defined, 78, 89; mother to child, 78–79, 89; wife to husband, 93–94; daughter to father, 98; daughter to mother, 102–03; sister to sister, 107–08; sister to brother, 114–15; training and adult behavior, 128

Drunkenness: attitude toward, 93, 114; as subject for joking, 95–96, 105; as subject for reprimand, 105, 121

Dyadic relationships: source of data, 87–88; interview techniques used, 87–89; methods of categorizing, 88–89; categories, 89–90; processing the data, 90; findings, 90–129; wife to husband responsibility, 90–93; wife-to-husband dominance, 93–94; wife-to-husband succorance, 94; wife-to-husband nurturance, 94–95; wife-to-husband obedience, 95; wife-to-husband aggression, 95–97; daughter-to-father responsibility, 97–98; daughter-to-father dominance, 98; daughter-to-father succorance, 99; daughter-to-father nurturance, 99–100; daughter-to-father obedience, 100; daughter-to-father aggression, 100–01; daughter-to-mother responsibility, 102;

daughter-to-mother dominance, 102–03; daughter-to-mother succorance, 103–04; daughter-to-mother aggression, 104–06; sister-to-sister responsibility, 106–07; sister-to-sister dominance, 107–08; sister-to-sister succorance, 108–09; sister-to-sister nurturance, 109–10; sister-to-sister obedience, 110; sister-to-sister aggression, 111–13; sister-to-brother responsibility, 113–14; sister-to-brother dominance, 114–16; sister-to-brother succorance, 116–17; sister-to-brother nurturance, 117–118; sister-to-brother obedience, 118–19; sister-to-brother aggression, 119–21; problems of interview techniques, 121–24; summary of findings, 121–29; child-training and adult behavior, 124–29

Earthquakes: mentioned, 9–10
Economic data. See Socioeconomic data
Eggan, Fred: on Philippine studies, 3–4; mentioned, 128
Erasmus, Charles J.: on classification of village activities, 25–26
Esperanza (Leyte): village studies, 68
Evangelista, Alfred: on kin relationships, 65

Fallers, L. A.: on concept of family, 62
family, types: nuclear, 48; categories of, 48–62; intact nuclear, 48, 50–53; truncated nuclear, 48, 53–54; re-established nuclear, 48, 54; extended horizontal, 48, 54; extended vertical, 49, 55–58; skipped generation extended vertical, 49, 58; truncated (residual), 49, 58–59; idiosyncratic, 49–50, 59
Farmers: tenant, 32–33, 70; classified as occupational group, 33–34; relation to land ownership, 37–39; relation to cash income, 39–40. See also Agriculture
Fathers: age of, 50–52; role as disciplinarians, 80; role with daugh-

ters, 97–101. See also Dyadic relationships; Kin relationships
Field work, problems in: selection of data, 7–8
Fieldworker: special problems of, 7–8
Filipinos: origins, 16; systems of government, 16
Fischer, John L.: on village residence types, 60; mentioned, 128
Fishermen: as largest occupational group, 33; relation to land ownership, 37–38; relation to cash income, 39–40; relation to social classes, 43; mentioned, 70
Fishing: as economic activity, 26, 27; mentioned, 3
Fish vendors: as occupational group, 33; relation to land ownership, 37–38; relation to cash income, 39–40
Food, securing: as wife-to-husband responsibility, 91; as daughter-to-father responsibility, 98; as daughter-to-mother responsibility, 102
Footwear, described, 20
Fortes, Meyer: on composition of domestic groups, 62
Furniture, described, 21

Gocan, village of: mentioned, 15
Goodenough, Ward H.: on village residence types, 60
guerrillas: mentioned, 13, 14
Guinhangdan (not real name) (Leyte): selected for investigation, 3–8; as agricultural-fishing village, 3, 33; position and description, 9–10, 12; history and settlement, 10–13; during World War II, 13–15; as rural barrio, 16; schools, 16, 18; government of, 16, 18; type of clothing worn in, 18–20; type of housing, 18, 20–22; socioeconomic structure, 23–44; work patterns, 26
Guthrie, George M.: on differences in child-rearing attitudes, 83

Herskovits, Melville: on work, 25
Homans, G. C.: on kinship terminology, 69
Hongkong, 9

Horizontal family: defined, 49; described, 54
Household activities: as economic classification, 26
Households, data on: criteria used in defining, 29–30, 45, 50–59, 60–61; data, sources of, 45–47; methods used in data-processing, 47–48, 61–62; types of, 47–62; distribution of members, 48; methods of analyzing data, 48–50; findings, 50–59; need for analysis, 59; factors considered in analysis, 59–63; distinct from families, 60–61; concepts in determining, 60–63
Housing: described, 20–22; in Guinhangdan, 22; *photograph*, ff. 23; mentioned, 10–11, 18
Hunting: as economic activity, 26

Idiosyncratic family: defined, 49–50; described, 59
Illness: as wife's responsibility, 91–93; feigned, 95, 104; as daughter's responsibility, 98, 99, 102; as sister's responsibility, 107, 109
Iloilo: mentioned, 19
Income, cash: range of, 35–37; methods of obtaining, 36–37; relation to occupation, 39–40; as criteria in social classification, 41–44
Income data: as criteria in selecting informants, 6
Informants: selection of, 5–6
Information-gathering: training assistants in, 7; methods of, 7
Interviewing: techniques, 7, 23–29, 69–70, 87–89, 122; problems in, 122–24

Japan: during World War II, 13–15, *see* Occupation; trade with, 19; mentioned, 9
Joking: as form of discipline, 80; in behavior patterns, 95–97, 99, 117; common sources of, 95–96, 100–01, 104–05; compared with teasing, 96–97; as form of aggression, 100–01, 104–05, 111, 119–20

Kin relationships: defined, 64–65; terminology, 65–69; created by marriage, 65, 67; artificial systems, 65, 67; sponsor system, 67–68; compared with American patterns, 69; mother to child, 69–86
Kroeber, A. L.: on kinship terminology, 66

Laborers: as occupational group, 33; defined, 33; relation to land ownership, 37–38; relation to income, 39–40; relation to social class, 43; mentioned, 27, 70
Land: size of holdings, 31; tenancy farming, 31–33
Land owners: mentioned, 25
Land ownership: as criteria in selecting informants, 6; difficulty of establishing accuracy, 24; as index to socioeconomic standing, 27, 30; as compared to house ownership, 30–31; relation to occupation, 37–39; relation to social class, 41, 43
Land use: described, 31, 32–33
Language: problems in communication, 7
Levy, M. J., Jr.: on concept of family, 62
Leyte: Japanese invasion of, 13–15; studies in, 68; mentioned, 4, 9, 10
Leyte Gulf: mentioned, 10
Longevity, 56–57
Luzon: migration from, 12; mentioned, 9, 10, 13
Lynch, Frank: studies of social rank, 41, 42; on kin relationships, 65; mentioned, 228

Manila: mentioned, 9, 10, 23
Mariana Islands, 9
Marriage: as residence system, 65; in system of kinship, 65, 67; in changing responsibility of daughter to father, 98; daughter to mother, 102; as source of joking, 105; sister to sister, 107; brother to brother, 114, 117
Matronymic naming: problem in census data, 46–47
Men: clothing worn, 19–20; work patterns, 25–26; occupations, 25–44. *See also* Dyadic relationships; Fathers; Kin relationships
Middle class: criteria used in defining, 42–43

Mindanao, 9
Money: as index to socioeconomic standing, 27; responsibility of wife, 91, 95, 96; of daughter, 98, 99, 102; need of, 99, 103, 116; mentioned, 105, 109, 117
Moneylenders: mentioned, 25, 28
Mother - to - child relationships: sources for data, 69–70; succorance training, 71, 72–73, 82; personality a factor, 71; achievement training, 73, 74–76, 82; responsibility training, 74, 75–76, 82; standards for, 76; obedience training, 76–77; sociability training, 77–78; dominance training, 78–79; aggression training, 78–79; forms of punishment, 79–80; teasing, 79–80; in disciplining, 80; forms of rewards, 81–82; standards demanded in behavior, 82; independence-dependence, 82–83; summary of findings, 82–86; questionnaire form for study, 131–39
Murdock, George P.: on primary relatives, 64

Names, use of: in tracing households, 17
Nipa palm: in housing, 21; *photograph*, ff. 23; sewing, 27; in land use, 31; thatch weavers, 33; mentioned, 10, 93, 109, 114. *See also* Palm-thatch weaving
Nuclear family: described, 48–54
Nurturance: in dyadic relationships, 89; defined, 89–90; in illness, 92; wife to husband, 94–95; daughter to father, 99–100; daughter to mother, 103, 106; sister to sister, 109–10, 113; sister to brother, 117–18

Obedience: defined, 76, 90; mother to child, 76–77, 83–84, 89; compared, 82–84; to elders, 84; dyadic relationships, 90; wife to husband, 95; daughter to father, 100, 101; daughter to mother, 104, 106; sister to sister, 110, 113; sister to brother, 113–14, 118–19; training and adult behavior, 127; to siblings, 127–28; mentioned, 111

Occupation of Philippines: Spanish, 12–13; mentioned, 16; Japanese, 13–15; mentioned, 24
Occupations: problems in classifying, 25, 26; patterns in, 26; as index to socioeconomic standing, 27; criteria in defining, 27–28; methods of gathering data, 28–29; distinctions in, 33; classified by size, 33; classified by types, 33–35; kinds and frequency, 34–35; relation to land ownership, 37–38; relation to income, 39–40; as criteria in social classification, 41–44; social ranking compared with America, 42
Oiling, technique of: described, 93, 99, 103–04, 117; mentioned, 103 104
Orphan, defined in Philippine society 53
Outrigger canoes: mentioned, 5, 7, 10, 20, 109

Pal, Agaton P.: on age and sex roles, 68–69
Palm-thatch weaving: as occupation, 33; in relation to land ownership, 37–38; in relation to cash income, 39–40; in relation to social class, 43
Palo (Leyte): mentioned, 10, 18, 19, 23
Parents: cultural responsibility toward, 99–100, 102; treatment of elderly, 99, 104, 105
Patronymic naming: problem in census data, 47
Pensioners: as occupational group, 34; relation to land ownership, 37–38; relation to cash income, 39–40; relation to social classification, 43
Personality: a factor in mother-child relationship, 71
Philippine Islands: anthropological investigations of, 3–4; described, 9–10
Philippines: as republic, 15; school system, 16; health services in, 16; agriculture, 16
Población: defined, 15–16
Primary relatives: defined, 64

Punishments: forms of, 79–80; who administers, 80–81; mother to child, 80; father to child, 80; by siblings, 80–81, 84–85, 115

Quarreling: in behavior pattern, 92, 93–94, 95, 99, 109

Relationships, within household: methods of obtaining information, 45–47; methods used in classifying, 48–50; age as factor, 50–52; primary, defined, 64; secondary, defined, 64; tertiary, defined, 64. *See also* Kin relationships
Religion: in behavior patterns, 91, 92, 101, 106, 112
Reprimand: defined, 97; sources of, 101, 105, 106, 112, 121
Residual family. *See* Truncated family
Responsibility: defined, 74, 89; mother to child, 74–76, 89; of wife, 90–93; of husband, 91, 92–93; daughter to father, 97–98; daughter to mother, 102; sister to sister, 106–07; sister to brother, 113; training and adult behavior, 125–27
Rewards, forms of: mother to child, 81–82, 85; from others, 85; compared, 85
Rice farming: *photograph*, ff. 23; in land use, 26, 31; as occupational classification, 33; mentioned, 14, 93
Romani, John H.: on barrios, 15, 16
Ropemakers: as occupational classification, 34; relation to land ownership, 37–38; relation to cash income, 39–40; relation to social class, 43. *See also* Abaca

Schneider, D. M.: on kinship terminology, 69
Schoolteachers: in Guinhangdan, 18; as occupational classification, 35; in relation to land ownership, 38, 40; in relation to cash income, 39–40; in relation to social class, 43; mentioned, 70
Scolding: defined, 97; as social discipline, 97; daughter to father, 101; to mother, 106; of sister, 110, 112–13; mentioned, 109
Sex, role: and age, 68–69; of women, 92
Shoes. *See* Footwear
Sibley, Willis E.: mentioned, 18
Siblings: a factor in child training, 72, 73; as disciplinarians, 80–81, 84–85; considered in processing data, 90; care of, 92; attitude toward older, 106–07, 113, 115–16, 119, 121; dominance patterns, 107; scolding, 110; aggression in, 112; relationship of, 114, 117, 119
Sitio: defined, 12, 15
Size and range of families: intact nuclear, 52; extended vertical, 55
Sociability: defined, 77; mother to child, 77–78, 84, 89; compared, 84
Social stratification: criteria used in defining, 40–44; in defining a middle class, 42–43; criteria compared with American society, 44
Socioeconomic data: use of census, 23; sources, 23–29; methods of processing, 29; findings, 29–44
Spanish: occupation of Philippines, 12–13, 16
Spanish-American War: mentioned, 13
Sponsor system. *See* Kin relationships
Stoodley, Bartlett H.: on authority of siblings, 80–81
Store owners: as occupational group, 35; relation to land ownership, 37–38; relation to cash income, 39–40
Succorance: mother to child, 71, 72–73; wife to husband, 94; daughter to father, 99; daughter to mother, 103–04, 106; sister to sister, 108–09, 113; sister to brother, 116–17; compared with dominance, 116; training and adult behavior, 125; mentioned, 7
Suki. See Debt

Tacloban (Leyte): mentioned, 4, 10, 12, 13, 19, 23
Tagalog: mentioned, 12, 80, 81
Tanuan (Leyte): mentioned, 10
Teachers. *See* Schoolteachers

Teasing: defined, 79; as social discipline, 79–80; in mother-child relationship, 80; compared with joking, 96; as reprimand, 96–97; in daughter-father relationship, 100–01; in daughter-mother relationship, 105; in sister-to-sister relationship, 111; in sister-brother relationship, 120
Tirykian, Edward A.: studies in social rank, 42; mentioned, 128
Truncated family: defined, 48–49; described, 58–59
Typhoons: mentioned, 9–10

United States: administration of Philippines, 13; occupation by, 14; trade with Philippines, 19

Vertical family: defined, 49; described, 55–58
Vietnam: mentioned, 3
Villages: near Guinhangdan, 10
Visayan Islands, 3, 10

Visiting customs, 22

Walay dialect, mentioned, 68
Waray Waray: use in interviews, 7, 69, 88; dialects compared, 68; mentioned, 12, 37
Whiting, Beatrice B.: on child-training practices and personality, 71–72
Whiting, John M.: on interview schedule, 69; on personality, 72; on socialization of child, 87; on behavior systems, 89
Women: age as parents, 50–52; unmarried, 57; interviewed, 69–70, 87–89, 122–23; relation to children, 69–86; duties, 90–93, 95, 96, 98, 102. *See also* Childbirth; Dyadic relationships; Marriage; Mother-to-child relationships; Work
Work: *photographs*, ff. 22, 23; patterns of, 25–27; of wives, 92–93; of husbands, 93–94; of daughters, 98, 102